It's Not the Tech:

Leadership Lessons from the I.T. Field

By Richard Blalock

Richard Blalock

ISBN: 979-8-3359-6355-8

Published by Richard Blalock

This is a work of non-fiction. Names, characters, businesses, places, events, and incidents have been modified to be used in a fictitious manner. Any resemblance to actual persons, living or dead, or actual events is purely coincidental.

Printed in the United States of America

Richard Blalock

Table of Contents

Acknowledgements

First, to my loving and caring wife Amber, who spent countless hours helping me compose my thoughts and perspectives onto these pages, who encouraged me to put this out there and take the step to actually release a book, who took the time to read and provide her thoughts and input throughout, who stayed up late with me talking over various concepts and ideas that should be shared. I love you more than I can articulate in writing.

To my daughter Sara, who – when told what the subject of the book was about, commented that it was "the most boring topic ever".

To my son Joseph, who agreed that it was very "skibidi", whatever that means.

To my colleagues and team members past and present – especially those in the OCE – thanks for making work fun, and just for being the amazing people that you are. I appreciate each and every one of you.

To my friends and colleagues with the CITMF – particularly Brett, Heather, Jeannette, Snorri, Mike, and others – thanks for taking me under your wing and helping me throughout all those years.

To Mr. Cecil, my first Computer Science teacher and mentor at COS, thanks for getting me interested in the I.T. field!

To Matthew (NOT Matt), thanks for being my first reader of the book, for finding typos that I missed, and providing great encouragement and feedback.

To the guys at the IC and particularly Team Bravo – thanks for the wisdom, encouragement, and accountability. Bit by bit.

To Brian and Anthony – thanks for putting up with my late-night streams of consciousness in our voice chats.

PART I:
REFRAMING

I've had the privilege of working in I.T. for 20 years – nearly my entire adult life. Throughout my career, I've navigated various roles and environments, from managing a one-person I.T. department to being part of small teams and working in large, complex enterprise settings. This journey has brought me face-to-face with a myriad of interesting, difficult, frustrating, and sometimes humorous situations, many of which I share within these pages.

Each chapter begins with a real story drawn from my experiences. These stories span diverse fields, including healthcare, finance, retail, law, and the public sector. The anecdotes and quotes are written to convey the essence of the conversations and lessons learned. While they may not be perfect and are influenced by the passage of time and memory, the core principles and insights remain intact. To protect privacy, the names, organization types, and other non-substantive details have been altered.

If you're not an I.T. professional and are already questioning why you're reading this book, I encourage you to stick with me. The lessons learned and strategies shared in the upcoming chapters are universally applicable to nearly every area of leadership. Don't worry, I won't bore you with overly technical lingo or leave you feeling lost.

Thanks again for reading this book. I hope it inspires you in your leadership journey!

- Richard

Chapter 1:
The Problem

I pulled up to the parking spot of the office and took a deep breath. *"OK, here we go. You got this."* I stepped out of the car, checked my appearance in the window reflection, and confidently walked into the office building. This was my first (real!) I.T. job, working for a technical support company that provided both one-time and ongoing support to homes and small businesses. My first assignment was to set up services for a brand new client, a consulting firm with a few regional offices in my area. It was my first week on the job, and I wanted to start off on the right foot by building a good relationship with our new customers.

I was scheduled to meet the outgoing "I.T. guy" – who, I was told, had provided support to the company for almost 10 years. He was now retiring, and the consulting firm opted to outsource services to my company rather than hire someone new.

Good morning, I'm Richard, I'm here to meet with (*Henry*)."

The administrative staff at the front desk looked me up and down, then gave me an awkward smile. "Right, yes, he's…. outside." She got up and walked me down the corridor of offices to the back of the building, opened the door, and pointed to a camper trailer sitting alone about 30 feet away under a canopy of trees. "You'll find Henry in there".

Well, this is weird, I thought to myself, but thanked the kind receptionist, walked to the trailer, and reached up to knock on the door.

"It's open!" came a reply from inside.

I pulled the creaky door open, and stepped into the musty, dark trailer. As my eyes adjusted, I took a quick look around. I saw stacks of various food boxes on the small kitchen counter, piles of clothes lying around on the floor, and a lava lamp sitting on a shelf. Looking over, I found what must have been his "workspace" – the combination couch and dining table area of the trailer, with 2 old monitors sitting on top of a few books stacked together. A musty smell hit my nose – a mixture of dust and burnt electronics. A small radio on the shelf was playing lo-fi music, but the speaker was cheap, and the sound came out tinny.

The man inside was wearing an oversized t-shirt, with some anime character pasted on the front. His hair was unkept, his baggy jeans held up by a belt with a chain going around back to his wallet. He gave me a friendly smile and reached out his hand, saying "So, you're the guy they hired to replace me, huh?"

"Guilty as charged." I chose to take the friendly route.

"Well, all for the best. They never really listened to me, so it will be your problem now. Take a seat, and I'll show you the mainframes that you'll be maintaining."

Mainframes? I don't know mainframes! The imposter syndrome began creeping in. Was I really qualified to do this? I had recently completed my associate degree in computer science, while making a small amount of money being the "computer guy" for people in my community. But I had no idea what he was talking about. Pushing back self-doubt, I smiled back and asked where I should sit.

He shuffled ahead of me, pulled a basket of laundry off the couch and – I kid you not – swept away two bags of chips, along with their crumbs, off the keyboard and onto the floor.

"This environment is very complicated", he said, narrowing his eyes at me while pushing his glasses up higher. "It will take a lot of work to support the databases and email system, otherwise things will go bad fast". I hesitantly sat down next to him, slid my laptop out from the bag, and set it on the edge of the table.

We spent the next hour reviewing the environment and the work that my company would be taking over. Truth be told, I could have learned everything I needed to from this guy in about 15 minutes. It turns out the "mainframe" was just a windows computer hosting files, the "databases" were just simple network drives that staff connected to which held those files, and the "email system" was an old, hosted email service provided by the local internet company. No mainframes, no databases, nothing crazy or advanced at all.

I ended my meeting with Henry and stepped down from the trailer, feeling my blood pressure lower with each step. I felt confident that I could support this company – my biggest problem was figuring out what issue to tackle first! The walk back into the main office was refreshing, breathing in fresh air after sitting in that dusty, dark trailer.

My next meeting was with the owner of the company. I was excited to get to know him and gain an understanding of his company's needs. I wanted to learn what was working well, and – more importantly, what wasn't going so well. Based on my meeting with Henry, I braced myself for an interesting discussion.

I went back to the friendly receptionist and told her I was ready to meet with the owner. She picked up the phone, punched in some buttons, and said "Richard is ready to speak with you", before hanging back up, looking at me, and giving me a smile. "Mr. Smith is ready for you, go on in", pointing to a door in the hallway. I walked down the hallway, pausing to again check my reflection in the mirror. My collared shirt had wrinkled a bit – sitting in the cramped trailer would be the cause of that. I only hoped that the smell hadn't stuck to my clothes as well.

I opened the door to see the owner of the consulting firm – a wiry man in his mid-50s, wearing business casual attire (similar to what I was wearing). He stood up from behind his L-shaped wooden desk and looked me up and down. "Oh, yes, I'm (Brett). Pleasure to meet you."

After exchanging pleasantries, I dove right in – I was eager to hear his perspective of things. My first question – "How have things been with Henry?

"How much time do you have?" he exclaimed, rolling his eyes and waving his hands in the air in frustration. We spent the next half hour going over the litany of issues the organization had been experiencing over the past several years. First, their email would randomly stop working several times a month, with the program giving the error that it would not connect to server. "We'd call him for help, and he would tell me he'd work on it, but sometimes it would take several hours or even days! Some of my team members would just use their personal email accounts instead for urgent tasks".

He also mentioned that many staff members had complained to him about files that had gone missing from their network drives. They would call Henry, but he was never able to help find the files, let alone restore them from previous backups. "I don't know where the backups are, or how we can even get to them if we need them! There are years of critical business files on those servers, and I really don't have any idea how it all works. Anytime I'd ask him, he'd launch into some gibberish about databases or something? I don't really know…it's always been something we needed to get sorted out, we just never got around to it."

I then heard how slow their computers were, and how they would frequently call Henry for support. Their issues included random lockups, freezes, blue screens, and overall poor performance, which Brett indicated would be a constant issue. "My staff would call him for help, but he had to come onsite to each office to look at the computer. Other companies I've seen – their techs can remotely connect to their computers and help them out faster. Why can't we do that?"

We spent a few minutes discussing my company's approach, some changes I think we should make, and – more than anything – reassuring the owner that he was now in good hands. I was confident that Henry was not taking care of these good folks in any meaningful way. If anything, he was taking advantage of their lack of technical knowledge to get away with poor performance.

As he walked me out of his office, we shook hands. "I have to admit", he said, looking me up and down. "You're not what I expected. I guess I figured all you techs would be relatively the same – kind of... grungy looking and socially awkward."

Returning the handshake, I smiled, and said the first thing that came to my mind: "It's a new day."

WHAT IS HAPPENING?

This was my first insight into some of the real problems organizations face in handling their I.T. needs — a pattern that persists to this day, nearly two decades later. I can't tell you how many times I've had someone tell me "I don't have a clue what they do" or "I have no idea how they're spending their time" when talking about their tech support. Many leaders have confided in me, secretly admitting that they just accept the information provided by their I.T. staff, given their inability to tell if it's true or false.

To be fair, it's important to recognize that for organizations with dedicated I.T. staff, regardless of their size (whether one person or 20+), the head of the technology department typically reports to a non-technical individual. This can be an operations manager, a deputy director, or general manager of the company. Of course, these leaders have other areas of responsibility – many of which they went to school for – such as human resources, budgeting, project management, facilities management, or others. It is unreasonable to expect nontechnical leaders to have the depth of understanding to correct a subordinate I.T. Manager. For example, should an operations manager of a consulting firm that provides accounting services know what DNS is, and why it's causing issues for their network? Of course not! All they know is that they can't connect to their network, their operations are negatively impacted, and they need it fixed ASAP.

Unfortunately, too many I.T. staff have taken advantage of their manager's lack of technical knowledge, exploiting this ignorance to produce shoddy, unprofessional, or overpriced work. As a result, companies are faced with reduced quality, increased costs, and an erosion of trust between I.T. and the rest of the organization.

Throughout my career, I've encountered various situations – both personally and through stories from colleagues – that shed light on various failures within I.T. departments. One example was told by my friend, who accepted a new position in I.T. management, replacing the previous leader who was with the company for over 20 years. As my friend was settling into her new workspace, she discovered that her predecessor had re-wired the backup internet line (which is only supposed to be used for major failures) from the network closet directly into his office. This gave the previous manager open, unfiltered internet access to play video games (or worse?). Another friend (non-technical) shared how their I.T. team member would disappear for hours or even days on end, telling each regional office that he was at the other office.

On further investigation, it was discovered that he was actually back at home, and not working at all.

These issues can also impact a company's bottom line. One I.T. director decided they needed a "very high end" (overpriced) laptop to support the office. This manager was later caught using the laptop to play video games during company time. A friend also shared the story of a systems administrator that was found to be mining bitcoin on company servers. This wasn't discovered for several months and was causing the company to pay increased utility costs, as well as reduced performance in the application hosted on the server. Another contracted technician was found to be charging excessively high fees for very simple services. Upon further investigation, it was found they were exaggerating the time it would take to accomplish basic tasks.

These issues could potentially fall into questionable areas of fraud or legality. For example, one I.T. contractor convinced their client that they needed to purchase new computers for all users, even though the existing computers were relatively new and in good condition. The contractor arranged for the company to buy the replacement workstations from a specific vendor, who then provided a kickback to the contractor.

While some of these examples may seem minor or even humorous at first glance, the reality is that these instances of misconduct by technical staff are actually breaches of trust and responsibility. As a result, an organization's budget, stability, security, and productivity are all impacted. These failures also erode the trust between these staff members and the organization's leaders, limiting their ability to innovate and collaborate on new ideas or solutions.

Ask yourself: have you ever found yourself in a new I.T. role within an organization, questioning the decisions of your predecessor and wondering, "*What were they thinking?*" Or, as an organizational leader, have you ever glossed over at the overly technical language used by your I.T. staff as they're discussing issues? Lastly, for those in I.T. roles, can you honestly say you've *never* exaggerated a situation when communicating with non-technical colleagues, even if only slightly, to smooth over a mistake you made?

At first glance, the examples I shared earlier may appear to be technical issues or failures. But a deeper look tells a different story. The guy mining bitcoin on servers – this wasn't a technical issue; it was misuse of company property. The manager re-routing the internet line for personal use – this is really a staff member disregarding company protocol and misuse of their infrastructure. The I.T. director who bought a gaming laptop reveals a broader issue of financial management and lack of accountability in the organization.

When you take a step back, it becomes evident that none of the issues I shared are technical in nature. These aren't I.T. failures, they come from a different source altogether. The stories I shared are more obvious instances, but there are also more subtle challenges people face. It's the company that commits to a new software product without fully understanding their needs. It's the organization that is stuck in their ways, because "that's how we've always done it". It's the I.T. guy that communicates in overly technical jargon to a non-technical audience. It's the manager that fails to properly budget for the future of the department and cannot replace aging and failing hardware.

This is a book about leadership, but more specifically, it's a guide to help you navigate the challenges of leading in our rapidly advancing digital age. At the core of effective leadership lies the ability to solve problems, and the first step in any problem-solving process is to define the problem. Too often, people have approached their technical challenges from a narrow perspective, focusing solely on the surface-level issues. In this book, we will shift our focus to reveal the underlying issues that afflict I.T. departments worldwide.

Each chapter will conclude with a set of key takeaways, summarizing the principles and insights for easy future reference. While the context of this book is rooted in technology leadership, the lessons are universally applicable across diverse scenarios and industries. Whether you're a seasoned I.T. veteran, a new leader stepping into a role overseeing a team of technical professionals, or an executive responsible with overseeing the I.T. department within your organization, this book is designed to offer practical strategies and perspectives to empower you to deal with the real issues in I.T.

My hope is that this book serves as a valuable resource, empowering leaders across organizations of all sizes to evolve their approach to technical challenges. By recognizing that technology is rarely the sole issue and embracing a new understanding of the complexities at play, you'll be equipped to navigate the hurdles of the digital era with confidence. In the next chapter, we'll identify and outline the real problem (and it's not the tech). The following chapters will then outline specific areas that we as leaders can hone in on to improve our ability to successfully navigate our organizations. So, buckle up, and let's embark on this transformative journey together!

Key Takeaways:

- **Exploitation of technical ignorance:** Many I.T. teams exploit the lack of technical knowledge in their users (and leaders), resulting in subpar work with minimal accountability.
- **Consequences:** Organizations suffer and can face financial or even legal consequences as a result of this exploited relationship.
- **It's not the tech:** Most I.T. failures are not technical in nature, but stem from other sources.

Chapter 2:
The Source

I was contacted by an old friend from high school who now manages a nonprofit summer camp that hosts events for various schools and religious groups. This particular camp holds a special place in my heart, as I attended several events there, many with my friend who later became the camp director. My childhood memories are filled with long sunny days at the lake and nights under the stars. We would hike through the woods, soaking in the smells and sights, pretending to be adventurers discovering new streams, caves, and hideouts. When it was too hot, we'd cool off in the lake, the icy water giving us goosebumps. At night, we would gather around the campfire, roasting marshmallows and swapping ghost stories. These experiences deeply influenced who I am today.

They had just purchased new camp management software (yes, those do exist) to help support their operations and asked if I could help them set it up. Primarily, the software would serve to automate the registration process, allowing attendees to register online, add any medical information, accept payments or setup payment plans, and sign waivers. My friend was thrilled at the possibility of saving a significant amount of time over their current (manual) methods. Additionally, they were excited at the solution's ability to accept payments for individual campers, rather than only take large lump sum payments from the church or school. This new functionality will allow families to pay directly for their own children. Knowing the great benefit the camp provides, I agreed to chip in and help.

Everything was running smoothly. My friend was thrilled with the new functions and quickly adapted to the updated processes. I joined regular check-ins between the camp and the vendor, and everything was being completed on schedule. They had just finished the first major phase of the project – to register campers through the software and were ready to begin phase 2 – the financial component. I reviewed the documentation provided by the vendor to familiarize myself and scheduled a virtual kickoff meeting.

The meeting was attended by camp leadership, implementation specialists with the vendor, and me, serving as the liaison between the two parties. At the beginning of the meeting, I described how they needed the software to be configured to be able to apply payments received to specific campers, as well as taking lump sum payments from schools and churches.

Then came the bombshell. "Oh, no – that's not possible," came the voice from the vendor's implementation specialist (*Mike*), spoken nonchalantly as if discussing the weather. I paused and looked up at my friends in the grid of faces filling the screen, seeing a mixture of confusion and frustration.

"What do you mean?" I pressed, keeping my voice steady despite the rising uncertainty.

"Our system can't do that". Mike reiterated, his tone final.

His answer sparked an immediate outcry from my friend. "Wait, hold up – that's not what we were told, your sales rep assured us that we could accept payments and apply them to individual campers!"

With emotions running high, the meeting quickly devolved into a tense back-and-forth exchange between camp staff and the vendor. Ultimately, it was determined that a core function that my friend needed from this software supposedly didn't exist. To make matters worse, they had already signed the contract and had paid the vendor. In simple terms, my friend was stuck between a rock and a hard place.

The following week, I took a two-hour drive up to visit my friend at the camp. We walked around the lake, and the memories rushed back in. I took in the sights of the towering ponderosa pine trees, the sounds of the flowing creek, and the smells of bear clover, and I was right back in my childhood again, blissfully enjoying the short walk. My friend, on the other hand, was a ball of anxiety, fearful over the investment he had made in the new software. As a relatively new camp director, he was mortified by the real possibility that he had wasted the nonprofit's tight purse strings on software that couldn't even do what he had envisioned.

As we walked along the lakeshore, we tried to come up with a way to make the new software work for them. A few ideas were proposed. Do we:

- Apply multiple payments from one large lump sum payment, manually adjusting each individual camper's file? (*"No, it would take too much time! We'd be better off manually processing things like we always have"*)
- Continue to take payments manually, and just use the new software for registrations only? (*"No, we picked*

this product specifically because we were told it could take payments for individual campers!")

- Pause the project and pay the vendor to expand their software to support this function? (*"No, we don't have the budget! We're a nonprofit!"*)

We were out of options and unsure how to move forward.

The following week, I joined the vendor for a review call. While looking through the program's administrative settings, I noticed one that was turned off – the setting was called "allow applying of payments to individual registrants".

"Hey Mike, what's that setting right there?" I asked.

There was a brief pause on the other end of the Zoom call. "Actually… I'm not sure. I've only been here a few years and never messed with that function".

Upon further testing – you guessed it! That setting *did* exist all along. I quickly called up my friend with the good news, and we got back on track. We completed the implementation, and they were able to fully use the software they had invested in. They appreciated the new features offered by the software, along with the enhanced and automated camper registration process.

THE CHASM

This wasn't the first time I ran into issues like this, and it wouldn't be the last. The gap between what organizations think they need and how they implement technology is growing – and will continue to do so as we increasingly rely on automated tools to save time and money. On a broader scale, this typically stems from a lack of collaboration between I.T. departments and the rest of their organization. Many teams invest in and try to deploy advanced solutions without fully engaging their I.T. teams to understand how (or if) these tools align with their actual needs. As a result, the new application, gizmo, or solution that was meant to simplify tasks, increase efficiency, and save money often ends up complicating things and increasing costs.

But was this the issue in the story I shared earlier? Fundamentally, the software could do what my friend needed it to do. In this case, the problem didn't originate from the technology itself but rather from the vendor's lack of understanding of their own product.

Let's imagine for a moment that the software did indeed lack that crucial feature. What would happen to my friend who ran the camp? In all likelihood, they would find themselves losing time and overspending on the project, or worse, having to throw money down the drain without any significant benefit. But is this a technical problem? Not quite. It's worth noting that my friend had researched and evaluated several products (there's actually a lot of camp management solutions out there, believe it or not) before settling on this particular one. They were well aware of the functionalities and differences among their options. They had placed their trust (and their money) in this solution to meet their needs.

My friend was fortunate in this scenario, but this instance underscores a fundamental challenge facing I.T. departments everywhere. The root cause didn't stem from the technology itself. Instead, it lied in their selection approach, the vendors insufficient training of their own staff regarding their own products, and the implementation procedures.

The reality is that the core challenges organizations face within their I.T. departments stem not from technological shortcomings, but rather from **people** and **process** shortcomings. More specifically, our I.T. problems stem from the **people** who are tasked to deploy, manage, and maintain the technology, and the **processes** that are in place to support their effective use.

Fundamentally, technology is merely a tool – and a tool's effectiveness is dependent on those who are wielding it and the systems in place to support its operation. Take, for example, a large professional sawmill. It is a powerful (and dangerous) tool that can only be effectively used by trained professionals. These professionals must be certified to operate the machinery after completing rigorous training programs and passing tests. The sawmill itself is supported by the building it's housed in, the electricity to power it, as well as water and other utilities to support it. The tool is supported by various parts and equipment to ensure it is running safely and efficiently. If, for example, a company ordered the wrong saw blade for this sawmill, is it the sawmill's fault? Or, if an untrained employee misused the sawmill and injured themselves or another person, do we blame the sawmill?

Looking back at the story told at the beginning of this chapter – if the software failed to meet my friend's requirements – does the fault lie with the technology itself? Of course not! There are many software products out there that could meet their needs. We're looking at the wrong thing here. Let's examine our story from the viewpoint of both the campground management, and the vendor:

First, for my friend, the director of the camp:

- Who was involved in the research and selection of the new software? (**people**)
- How thoroughly did they define their requirements before exploring available products? (**process**)
- What steps did they take to validate that the software they selected could do what they needed it to do? (**process**)
- Did they anticipate any procedural changes needed for transitioning to a new software solution? (**process**)
- Did they validate with other camp leadership to ensure that the chosen solution met their needs? (**people** and **process**)

Now for the vendor:

- How are they assigning the right staff that are most knowledgeable about their product? (**people**)
- What measures are in place to ensure that their staff are adequately trained to support customers effectively? (**process**)
- Why was Mike, the representative assigned to support the product, unaware of this particular function? (**people** and **process**)

When you take a deeper look, you'll find that most technology issues aren't inherently technical. Whether it's mismanagement of resources, ineffective communication, ambiguous organizational goals and objectives, insufficient training, or inadequate planning – the list is extensive. Regardless of the specific cause, you'll discover that the challenges confronting I.T. departments predominantly stem from **people** or **process** issues (or both).

Let's look at a few hypothetical examples:

- Several users have been complaining about slow computer performance in the office. But how old are the computers? If they need replacing, is that planned and budgeted for? (**process**) Are the users trained in best practices for using their computers? (**process**) Have the IT staff sat down and worked with end users to address their issues in real time, effectively communicating how they could improve performance (**people**)

- A user complains about multiple accounts with different passwords. She calls the I.T. helpdesk at least once a month for assistance with a password reset. But how has I.T. worked with her? Are they simply resetting the password each time, or do they possess the necessary customer service skills to help the user solve the issue in the long term? (**people**) Does the I.T. department offer any sort of secure password storage solution to their staff? (**process**)

- An employee inadvertently gains access to the company's human resources folder, granting them the ability to view sensitive information for all staff. The employee shared this sensitive and confidential data with others, which led to a lawsuit. But how did they get the permission required to access the folder? (**process**) Does I.T. regularly check their file permissions to ensure there is no unauthorized access? (**process**)

I've met countless I.T. leaders that are amazing at what they do and are some of the smartest folks I've ever met. They are geniuses at analyzing technical problems and solving them and have amazed me with their technical know-how. But many fall short in the areas of **people** or **process** (often both). Maybe they're short, rude, or ineffective communicators. They might have a reputation that they don't work well with their colleagues. Perhaps they don't communicate well with their boss on the status of their projects or tasks. It could be that they're insisting on using the same methods as they did 10, 15, or 20 years ago, because "that's how we've always done it". Maybe they've neglected their own professional development (or the development of their team members). As technology rapidly evolved, their failure to invest in training and upskilling left them and their team members ill-equipped to handle new challenges or adopt emerging innovations.

I've had the privilege of participating in numerous interview panels to hire I.T. leaders – and through this experience, I've personally come to prefer a particular type of candidate. The candidates I love to interview (and hire) are those who demonstrate not only technical expertise but also a willingness to grow, embrace challenges, and communicate effectively. Those who show adaptability and demonstrate effective communication skills are the ones that stand out to me. These skills are not confined to the realm of information technology; they can be applied across all areas within an organization (more on recruiting great staff in chapter 6).

SHIFTED FOCUS

Leaders who fail to prioritize the **people** and **process** aspects of their roles often find themselves grappling with ineffectiveness and overwhelming challenges. These shortcomings manifest in various ways – including dissatisfied staff, outdated and ineffective methods, constant "busyness", unclear communication channels, project delays, bloated staffing, and budgetary challenges, among others.

On the inverse, leaders who understand and are equipped to tackle the underlying **people** and **process** challenges are more likely to be successful in their endeavors. Their staff are generally happy and feel supported and empowered. They are constantly looking for ways to improve their processes and have a good handle on their own time and schedule. They are great communicators, strategic thinkers, and forward minded. They invest in their own continuing education and encourage their team members to do the same. They are better organized, accomplishing projects on time and allocating staff effectively.

To be more specific, when referring to the **people** problems (or opportunities, depending on how you look at it), there are several facets to it, which include, but are not limited to:

- Practicing effective leadership – which involves effective communication, delegation, and strategic planning;

- Recruiting the right staff – those that align with the organization's values and goals;
- Cultivating a healthy and productive culture that fosters collaboration and innovation; and
- Swiftly handling any interpersonal conflict when it arises.

When talking about the **process** problems (or opportunities), this includes:

- Encouraging creative and out of the box problem solving approaches to address challenges;
- Empowering staff by providing them with the necessary tools and training to succeed in their roles; and
- Establishing a culture of experimentation and encourages employees to explore new ideas and methods.

Over the years, I've come to realize that prioritizing **people** and **processes** lays a solid foundation for addressing technological challenges more effectively. This book is dedicated to that very principle. As leaders, when we shift our focus from the surface-level issues and focus on identifying the underlying **people** and **process** problems, we gain greater clarity in solving these problems. By better understanding the **people** we lead and the **processes** we rely on, we unlock our true potential as leaders.

The emphasis on **people** and **process** extends beyond the field of information technology. Although my background is in technology leadership, the principles discussed in the upcoming chapters are universally relevant to all domains of business leadership. By embracing and implementing these strategies, you'll be equipped and empowered to lead your organization effectively, regardless of the industry or sector you operate in.

The next time you encounter a challenge, whether it's related to I.T. or any other aspect of your work, take a moment to ask yourself: "What is the root of the problem?" On closer examination, you'll often find that the issue can be attributed to either a **people** problem, a **process** problem, or a combination of both. By identifying the underlying source, you can then leverage effective **people-** and **process-**management strategies, which we will explore in the upcoming chapters, to address the issue more effectively and successfully.

In the next section (chapters 3-5), we will look at three critical skills necessary to effectively lead your team (communication, delegation, strategy). These skills are fundamental in any environment, and while they may be a refresher for some, I'd encourage you to revisit them, as they lay the ground work for the chapters that follow.

After that, we'll address the **people** problem head-on in chapters 6-8. We'll start by focusing on the crucial task of recruiting the right talent, outlining strategies for finding and hiring individuals who are the best fit for your organization. Next, we'll look at the importance of fostering a healthy organizational culture that promotes team success. Finally, we'll wrap up the section by looking at conflict, its sources, and some strategies to navigate difficult discussions.

Finally, we'll look at the **process** problem in chapter 9-11. First, we'll look at the mantra of "that's how we've always done it" (which we always hear in the I.T. field) and explore strategies to break away from this mindset. Next, we'll go over a leadership strategy centered on empowering the users we're assigned to support within our organization. Finally, we'll look at project management and the importance of embracing failures as learning opportunities, as well as ways to get more done in less time.

Now, let's explore how you can harness the power of **people** and **process** to become the best leader possible!

Key Takeaways:

- **Misguided investments:** Many organizations invest heavily in the newest technologies, while not addressing the core issues that they are struggling with.
- **Root causes:** Nearly all I.T. issues are not inherently tech-related, but rather stem from **people** and **process** problems.
- **Negative impacts:** By not focusing on the **people** and **process** problems in an organization, leaders are ineffective, inefficient, and unproductive.
- **Shift in mindset:** As leaders, by shifting our mindset to look at the **people** and **process** problems, we can get on the right path to successfully leading a productive and effective team!

It's Not the Tech

PART II: LEADERSHIP ESSENTIALS

In my experience advising I.T. leaders, I've found three fundamental skills that are critical to success: communication, delegation, and strategic planning. Whether you're inspiring to lead a team, just starting out in a leadership role or you're a seasoned manager, the next section of this book can serve as a crash course in essential leadership principles.

Before we dive in, I'd like to share some invaluable resources that have greatly influenced my own leadership journey. I highly recommend reading the following books, which offer excellent insights applicable to any leadership scenario:

- *Extreme Ownership* by Jocko Willink and Leif Babin
- *The Way of the Shepherd: Seven Secrets to Managing Productive People* by Dr. Kevin Leman and Bill Pentak
- *Multipliers: How the Best Leaders Make Everyone Smarter* by Liz Wiseman
- *Shackleton's Way: Leadership Lessons from the Great Antarctic Explorer* by Margot Morrell and Stephanie Capparell

There are a million different resources, frameworks, books, podcasts, videos, and courses out there that provide guidance and advice for leaders. I'm not looking to reinvent the wheel here, but I do think that there are some foundational principles we need to look at as we reframe the challenges facing I.T. departments. As a leader dedicated to continuous growth, I encourage you to make time for investing in your leadership skills by exploring these excellent books and other valuable resources.

While specific strategies and techniques may vary, the importance of communication, delegation, and strategic planning is universally emphasized by credible leadership coaches. By immersing yourself in these resources and actively practicing these critical leadership skills, you'll not only enhance your effectiveness as an I.T. leader but also lay the foundation for long-term success and growth in your career

.

Chapter 3:
Communication

A colleague and I were set to interview three candidates for a position we were looking to fill. We developed our questions, held a pre-meeting to review their applications ahead of time, and overall felt ready to get started (we'll discuss how to recruit great team members in chapter 6). This position interfaced with all the end users in our organization, so it was important that we found someone who could demonstrate excellent interpersonal skills.

Candidate #1 was on time, well dressed, and generally friendly during introductions. However, when asked about his technical experience, he chose to only provide generic, vague statements in his responses. My colleague and I attempted to draw out additional details about his past work to figure out if he would be a good fit, to no luck.

Candidate #2 was also punctual, dressed appropriately for the interview, and seemed polite and friendly enough. When we asked our opening question (something along the lines of "tell us about your experience and why you believe it's relevant to the position?"), he launched into an extremely detailed, long winded breakdown of his career history. He provided overly verbose insight into his specific work areas, giving unnecessary details about certain projects he completed in the past. We eventually had to interrupt him several minutes in, to allow us to move on to the other questions we had. The interview continued on in the same fashion, and we were unable to finish asking our set of questions in the allotted time.

Like the first two, Candidate #3 arrived early and was ready to go on time. Dressed in a nice suit, he shook hands enthusiastically and was pleasant throughout the interview. Unfortunately, when asked for specific examples of his work history, every single one of his answers outlined an accomplishment 10, 15, or even 20 years prior. We pressed him to give more recent examples after a few times, at which he gave some vague answers – but then immediately jumped back into his old experience.

At the end of the day, I looked wearily at my colleague. "None of these will work."

"I agree," she replied, putting her head into her hands. "What a mess. None of these guys would work for our staff – they'd either bore them to death with details, not talk at all, or - with the third guy – might not even be able to help since we couldn't figure out if he has any recent experience!"

We revisited the applicant pool and found a few more suitable candidates to interview. This time around, we were closely evaluating their ability to communicate effectively. Ultimately, we found a great team member who demonstrated both excellent technical and interpersonal ability – not only within the team, but also to his supervisor and end users.

WE CREATED THIS MESS

You probably don't need a book to remind you that communication skills are essential for any leadership position. You already know that. But here's the thing: in my experience, the I.T. field often falls short in this department. Big time. Negative perceptions of I.T. team members are often, unfortunately, well-deserved and accurate. Stereotypes always contain a certain amount of truth, and for I.T., the image of the "guy in mom's basement" often comes to mind when nontechnical staff refer to them. You know what I'm talking about, and probably have a picture in your mind of someone when reading this. This didn't just materialize from thin air – it's the result of years of overly-technical jargon, awkward social interactions, and an overall disconnect between I.T. and the rest of the organization.

But the tide is turning. As the next wave of I.T. professionals graduate and enter the workforce, they're bringing with them a new perspective shaped by today's high-tech world. Take my 13-year-old daughter, for example. She's a wizard when it comes to iPhone settings and configurations. Me? I'm more of an Android person myself. I have, on more than one occasion, called on her to help me fix an annoying problem I've had with a work-provided Apple device or referred various friends and family to her for assistance. She's able to explain things in a way that is understood by whoever she is helping (and she's not even interested in I.T.).

Imagine for a moment that you have been assigned to give a presentation to your entire office on the latest cybersecurity risks. You're excited for the opportunity to share your knowledge with such a large group of people and take the time to prepare your slides and talking points. Feeling motivated and excited, you launch into your talk by outlining the types of phishing and ransomware attacks. As you're going through your talking points, you look out at your audience and see many are glazing over or not paying attention. Others are discreetly checking their phones. It's obvious you've lost them. At the end of your talk, you ask if anyone has any questions and…. crickets.

While we all can recall a time that a presentation didn't go as planned, I'd argue that this scenario happens more often in the I.T. field than anywhere else. Simply put, how I.T. staff communicate needs to evolve. Knowing *how* to communicate is just as crucial as *what* you're trying to convey. When you shift your focus from simply sharing information to tailoring it appropriately for your audience, that's where the magic happens. This is especially true when I.T. leaders evolve from just "fixing the tech" to becoming strategic partners that empower an organization (more on that in Chapter 10 – "Empowering End Users")

CAN YOU HEAR ME NOW?

Before we dive into some specific strategies for communicating effectively, it's important to ensure that we are first exercising active listening. This is simply the practice of being fully engaged and focused on what is being said, making sure you understand what's being communicated, asking questions if necessary, and providing feedback. This helps to build trust with the person you are communicating with that you are engaged and interested in what they are sharing. As they say, "God gave you two ears and one mouth for a reason!" Whether you are interacting with one person, a small group, or a large audience, active listening builds trust and demonstrates genuine interest in the speaker. This will also ensure that you can fully engage with what's being shared, fostering a healthy exchange of ideas, thoughts, and perspectives.

Here's a list of essential listening skills that you can start using now:

- **Adapting communication styles:** Recognize that the communication style of the speaker may be different than your own. Embrace this difference rather than allowing it to impede healthy dialogue. By adjusting your approach in the discussion to align with their style, you'll establish an environment that encourages mutual understanding and receptiveness.
- **Empathy:** Being empathetic when listening involves engaging with the speaker's emotions, thoughts, and viewpoints. By working to understand their experiences, you can validate their feelings.

- **Nonverbal communication:** Pay attention to subtle queues in gestures, facial expressions, and body language. These signals can provide valuable context and insight into the speaker's emotions and intentions, expanding your understanding of the conversation.

Active listening is the cornerstone of effective communication – by demonstrating genuine interest you will build trust with the speaker. Embracing these skills can ensure that you're starting off on the right foot, which will also boost your ability to communicate back to the other party.

NOT WHAT YOU SAID, IT'S HOW YOU SAID IT

Now that we've looked at some effective listening skills, let's explore some strategies to sharpen your communication with others. Below is a list of techniques you can employ to help ensure your message resonates and hits home:

- **Empathy:** This is so important that I'm listing it again. By considering the perspectives and emotions of your audience, you can foster deeper connection and understanding. You know this because you're practicing active listening skills and empathy already, right?

- **Set Clear Objectives:** Clearly state the purpose or goal of your communication right from the start, ensuring that everyone stays focused on the desired outcome.

- **Clear and Concise:** Ensure that your message is clear and straightforward to avoid confusion and capture your audience's attention.

- **Confidence:** Displaying confidence through your tone, body language, and delivery builds trust and credibility in your message. Stand tall, make eye contact, and speak with conviction to assert authority and reinforce your key points.

- **Assertiveness:** While we should always respect differing viewpoints, it's important to assert your positions in a healthy way. Being assertive not only reinforces your ideas but also reinforces your confidence.

- **Adaptability:** I've given presentations that have gone completely off the rails with random questions that may or may not be related to what I'm trying to talk about. While this isn't ideal, a certain amount of flexibility in your communication can be good, depending on the dynamics of the situation and the audience. We can respond thoughtfully (because we're practicing active listening) to these questions and inquiries, which will help boost audience participation.

WHO ARE YOU SPEAKING TO?

As a leader, when considering how to communicate effectively, you must be able to tailor your approach and be flexible in your style - depending on *who* you're talking to:

- **Within your team:** Effective communication within your team goes beyond simply assigning tasks; it's about demonstrating an understanding of how their effort contributes to the broader goals of the organization. For example, if you're assigning a project or a task to a team member, talk about how its successful completion will align with the team's goals and how it advances the organization's vision. By emphasizing the "why" behind these tasks and projects, you are empowering your team members to see the bigger picture and instill a sense of purpose and ownership in their work. This not only clarifies expectations but can inspire greater commitment among your team. This is one component of a larger topic surrounding a healthy work culture, which we will look at in greater detail in chapter 7.

- **To Leadership:** You need to keep your boss informed – both to maintain alignment, and also to ensure that your team's efforts are recognized and supported. Build an understanding of your boss's communication style and adapt your approach accordingly. Some may prefer brief, concise verbal updates, while others may appreciate more detailed reports or regular check-ins. By proactively seeking feedback on your communication style and adjusting it to meet your manager's expectations, you will show commitment to effective collaboration and mutual understanding. Additionally, don't hesitate to ask clarifying questions to ensure that you fully understand their expectations and priorities. For example, if they prefer email updates, consider summarizing key points in bullet points for quick reference. If they prefer face-to-face meetings, come prepared with visual aids or progress reports to support the discussion.

- **End Users:** This is absolutely essential for any I.T. department to be successful. When working with end users, tailor your communication to their level of technical understanding to ensure that your message resonates and is actionable. For example, if you have to explain a new software feature or process change, consider the range of technical proficiencies in the audience (and if you don't know, don't be afraid to ask!). Some people may appreciate a detailed technical breakdown with step-by-step instructions, while others might prefer a high-level overview that shows the benefits and implications. By adopting a "user-centric" approach and presenting information in a format that maximizes understanding, you'll increase engagement with your project or task, promoting an overall positive user experience. Finally, be intentional to solicit feedback from your end users to identify any areas of improvement – this will demonstrate your commitment to continuous improvement and end user (customer) service.

ON PRESENTATIONS

At one time or another, you'll probably have to give a presentation. Whether you're giving training to end-users, providing an update to your team on a project's status, or briefing leadership on the status of the department, it's a fact of life in the I.T. world. In most organizations, presentation updates – whether in person, virtually, or a hybrid of both – leverage popular software tools to communicate important points and updates. While these solutions are great for visual aids and providing concise information, they should never be the primary method of communication. As Dwight Schrute once said in the famous television series *The Office*, "PowerPoints are the peacocks of the business world; all show, no meat." Programs like PowerPoint, Canva, Prezi, or Google Slides are great support tools, but shouldn't be leaned on too heavily.

I can't tell you how many presentations I've attended, where someone is droning on and on, reading – verbatim – from a PowerPoint slide deck. Any effective communication skills are thrown out the window because the audience is just reading the wall of text they see on the large projector screen or TV. Moreover, many presenters simply read the slides, then summarize the same point again. This is useless and a waste of everyone's time.

If you're going to use a presentation tool, I'd strongly recommend the following practices to maximize engagement and ensure your message is received effectively:

- **Avoid walls of text:** There's no limit to the number of slides you have to use. Break text-heavy information out into multiple slides.

- **Font and size:** Be sure the material is readable by the audience by testing it out in advance on a larger screen, if possible, standing towards the back of the room to verify it can be read. It might look good on your computer monitor when sitting at your desk but ends up looking drastically different on the presentation screen.

- **Bullet Points:** Remember, the slides are an aid, not a crutch. You should be leveraging the information on a page as an aid to communicate effectively to your audience. They should be engaged in both you as the presenter (using those great communication skills we talked about earlier), as well as the slides. Break up the walls of text into more succinct bullet points – speaking to them and expanding as needed.

- **One point at a time:** Rather than advancing to the next slide that contains several bullet points, causing the audience to miss out on important information you're sharing (since they're reading ahead on your slide), setup animations to have each bullet appear one at a time, keeping the audience engaged and focused.

- **Graphics:** When appropriate, add graphics and pictures for additional emphasis and added engagement.

- **Use notes:** Most presentation tools have an area where you can add notes for yourself (not visible to attendees), which can be helpful to stay on track and not miss any important points.

How you digitally present your information is just as important as how you communicate to your audience. By following these simple tricks, you'll be sure to ace your next presentation!

KEEP TALKING

Effective communication is a foundational pillar of leadership and includes not just the ability to convey messages clearly, but also to listen actively and empathetically. By honing in your listening skills and mastering effective communication practices, you can cultivate trust, promote an environment of collaboration, and drive success for your organization. Whether communicating to your team, to leadership, or to end users, you can use the strategies outlined here to tailor the message and ensure comprehension and engagement. Finally, by following the tips and tricks outlined for presentations, you can ensure your message hits home.

Our exploration into essential leadership skills is just beginning. In the next chapter, we'll go over the critical need for effective delegation, outline why some leaders hesitate to delegate, and provide strategies to overcome these barriers.

Key Takeaways:

- **Bad reputation:** I.T. leaders have a well-deserved reputation for struggling to effectively communicate with the rest of the organization.
- **Active listening:** Communication skills are a two-way street – practicing active listening will build trust with others and help your message hit home.

- **Effective communication:** Demonstrating empathy, clarity, confidence and assertiveness with your audience will help your audience receive what you are trying to convey.

- **Tailored communication:** Who you are communicating with is also important – whether it's to your team, leadership, or to end users, tailoring your style to both their preference and technical understanding is essential.

- **Presentation skills:** When giving presentations, be sure to use any tool as a visual aid, using it to reinforce what you are communicating, and never simply re-read the text on the screen.

Chapter 4:
Delegation

A few years into running my own technology consulting business, I was contacted by the president of a medium-sized real estate agency. She was just recently hired and was new to the organization. Her first order of business was to conduct an end-to-end review of all departments, including accounting, human resources, operations, marketing, and I.T. The I.T. team was fairly large given the size (6 staff supporting the remaining ~40).

During my initial meeting with the president, I inquired whether there were any specific concerns she had about the I.T. unit. "Well," she began, "I'm honestly not sure. I was never really much into tech, and in my last job I would just rely on what they told me was going on," she admitted with a sheepish look on her face.

"That's fine," I reassured her. "I don't know anything about the real estate business!"

I took a few moments to explain my approach to evaluating the I.T. department. Her biggest concern was a recent request to add an additional support staff member. Apparently, their team was overwhelmed with the workload and needed more staff to keep up. I agreed that the size of the department (6) relative to the overall size of the company (around 40) already seemed high and promised to take a look.

Careful of drawing conclusions too early, I went forward with my evaluation process. I met with several middle managers, all of whom reported excellent customer service and prompt response time by the technical team. Overall, everyone was happy with the level of service provided. They also felt like they had all of the tech devices they needed to perform their jobs, and they were in good working shape, being replaced on a proper schedule.

Their answers perplexed me. In previous engagements, I would hear horror stories (like the one I shared in chapter 1) about poor response, old or malfunctioning equipment (or a lack of equipment), bad response times, poor customer service, and an inability to effectively resolve issues when they arose. This situation, however, was the exact opposite.

Toward the end of the engagement, I had an opportunity to sit down and meet with the I.T. team. They were all friendly, considering my presence which could come across as threatening. We enjoyed lunch together, where I inquired about any ongoing problems, concerns, or issues. The only response they provided was the universal belief that they were overwhelmed, overworked, and needed additional staff to handle the workload.

Finally, I had a meeting with the I.T. Director himself (M*itch*). He had been with the company for almost 20 years, working his way up into his current leadership role, and was approaching retirement in the next year or so. I had hoped to use my time with him to learn how he oversees his team's projects and tasks – perhaps identifying ways to streamline processes or improve communication.

"So, how do you meet with your team members to help them prioritize what they're working on, and offer support?" (this is my typical opening question).

"Oh, I don't do that. Everyone just sort of…" Mitch paused, before continuing. "…does their work."

"Wait," I stopped him, trying to be polite. "What do you mean?"

"Well, we've got our network guy, and our server guy. They keep everything running fine. We've also got our techs who respond to requests for help." He smiled confidently, before adding, "I'm sure you heard from folks just how good we are."

"I have!" I replied, slightly confused. *How can a leader lead when he doesn't know what his team members are working on?* "OK, so tell me then Mitch, what does a typical day look like for you?"

"I typically answer the phone for support and help people out when they need it. We use an open line here that rings in everyone's offices, and whoever answers the phone first helps out the user who calls in."

Now we're getting somewhere, I thought to myself. "You don't have your helpdesk staff serve as the first level of response for help?"

"Oh no, you see, I don't really have time to delegate. We're much too busy for that. I'm more of a hands-on leader anyway."

I had figured out the issue. Sure, things were running well for the end users, but the reality behind the curtain was a mess. No communication within the team (Mitch should read chapter 3), and an I.T. Director who was unable (or unwilling) to delegate effectively. The pieces were starting to come together.

With the veil lifted, I began to see things from a different perspective. Senior level staff - who should be addressing their backup challenges on the servers - were instead busy handling basic helpdesk calls. Meanwhile, the main person assigned to do the helpdesk work ended up with a lot more free time than he would like. While each staff member had a defined role, they often ended up jumping into different responsibilities due to a lack of proper delegation.

I set out to create a plan to help out the president of the real estate company. I had to be careful in this situation – the I.T. team was well established, and several had communicated their intent to retire soon. Would they be open to changing how they've done things for so long, when they were so close to retirement? If we did implement changes now, requiring Mitch to begin delegating tasks (changing how the team spends their time), what if he chooses to retire early? What about the end users – who were all happy with the level of support – what would the impact be to them with these changes?

Given the other priorities that the company president had, as well as how happy everyone was with I.T., we opted to take a delayed approach. While changes to the team were needed, we concluded that doing so immediately would do more harm than good. Rather than pull the rug out from the current team, we worked to plan how the next I.T. director would oversee and delegate. We created a staffing plan that clearly defined the roles of the team, and identified how some positions could be consolidated – allowing the department to be more efficient with proper delegation of duties. Finally, the president was able to postpone hiring any additional staff until the director retired and was replaced with someone fresh who could perform an unbiased assessment and determine what the department really needed.

WHY DELEGATE?

It was impossible to say for certain what staffing levels my client needed, and this was due to Mitch's failure to delegate effectively. This story is not unique – any environment where a leader cannot delegate projects, tasks, or assignments to their team will eventually get messy (if it isn't already). A department struggling in this area will face several challenges, including:

- **Overwhelmed leaders:** Managers or directors may find themselves struggling with tasks and responsibilities, leading to stress and burnout. They also will struggle to have the time and capacity to focus on strategic priorities (more on strategy in chapter 5).

- **Decreased productivity:** Tasks may pile up or are left unfinished, as team members lack any clear direction or guidance (this is especially true in offices that aren't overstaffed)

- **Stifled growth and development:** Leaders who fail to delegate may end up hoarding specific tasks and responsibilities, leading to potential missed growth opportunities for team members to expand their skills.

- **Lack of collaboration and engagement:** Team members may feel underutilized and disengaged, impacting motivation and morale.

- **Missed opportunities for innovation:** By not effectively leveraging the diverse experience and perspectives of team members, leaders are missing out on their ability to foster creativity, collaborate, or innovate.

- **Work product quality:** By not delegating, tasks and assignments might be overlooked, rushed, or not complete.

Team members in these environments have communicated feeling overwhelmed and overworked. Additionally, senior leaders assigned to oversee I.T. operations find themselves lacking the essential information required to guide their subordinate managers.

On the other hand, when you have an I.T. leader that effectively delegates, the department can thrive and achieve peak efficiency. There are effective channels of communication – both internally and with senior leadership. Morale is higher, as team members feel valued and know how they're contributing to the organization (we'll explore the topic of work culture in chapter 7). Some specific benefits include:

- **Increased productivity:** Tasks are distributed appropriately, leveraging each team member's individual strengths and areas of expertise.
- **Improved morale:** Employees feel empowered to take ownership of their work, and the sense of autonomy and responsibility helps boost job satisfaction.

- **Enhanced collaboration:** By working together on shared projects and assignments, team members can leverage each other's skills and abilities, enhancing the collaboration in the department.

- **Development of skills:** New opportunities present themselves for team members to pursue professional growth and skill development. By entrusting staff with new responsibilities or challenges, I.T. leaders can help them expand their skill sets and advance their careers.

- **Strategic focus:** By effectively delegating work to team members, the I.T. leader can focus time on long-term planning, innovative ideas, organizational growth, and individual team member performance.

- **Empowerment and engagement:** I.T. leaders can establish a relationship rooted in trust, allowing team members to be fully engaged and accountable for their work.

- **Avoiding burnout:** Effectively distributing workloads among team members can help prevent them from becoming overwhelmed with their projects or tasks in support of a healthy work-life balance.

If you apply the perspective shift that we outlined in chapter 2 – you'll see that the challenges facing the real estate office in the story at the beginning of the chapter were – (surprise!) – not technical in nature. The shortcomings were actually **people** and **process** problems:

- Mitch was not communicating effectively with the president or his team, creating interpersonal challenges (**people**)
- Senior staff were assigned to handle junior-level tasks, causing a breakdown in the department's workflow and hierarchy (**process**)
- A lack of delegation resulted in team members performing tasks outside their normal areas of responsibility (**process**)
- There was no way to track the department's workload, hindering productivity and resource allocation (**process**)

HESITATION

Mitch's story of adopting a "hands on" approach is one that is common among many I.T. leaders, but it also reveals a pattern seen among those who are working their way up the technology career ladder. Traditionally, I.T. managers or directors often begin their careers in more junior-level roles, where they handle tasks like end user support, hardware and software maintenance, inventory management, or other "tier 1" tasks. However, once they transition into a leadership role, they often find themselves reverting to the same tasks they were doing earlier in their careers.

When asked about this, many have shared with me their struggles with *imposter syndrome* – a feeling of anxiety and inadequacy, even when they are successful or high-performing. This anxiety often manifests as a perceived pressure or need to know the "most" about I.T. in their department. After all, as the boss, shouldn't they know more than anyone else on their team?

The problem with this is that you weren't hired to *do the most* in your team. You were hired to *lead your team*. Sure, you probably have a certain level of experience and knowledge in all the areas you're now overseeing. But that doesn't mean that you must always be the most knowledgeable of all areas of I.T. – especially considering the rapid pace of change in the technology field. Just because you're getting a bit rusty in areas that you previously were a whiz in, doesn't mean that you're falling short. It means that you're dedicating your time and energy to a different area – specifically, leading and supporting your team.

Other leaders have expressed trust issues when delegating tasks. This is the old adage of "if you want something done right, do it yourself". This concern is valid and usually stems from past sour experiences. Perhaps they assigned a task to someone, and it didn't get done in time. Maybe it came back in poor quality. Or maybe they didn't get what they expected from the request – they had an idea in mind, but it didn't come out that way (but this could also be a communication issue, which we went over in chapter 3). As a result, they are hesitant to relinquish control and trust projects or tasks to others. The problem with this is simple – you can't do everything yourself, even if you think you know how to do everything yourself.

Think of a ship at sea. A ship has a captain. That captain undoubtedly has experience in many areas of a ship. Perhaps he was a navigator, or maybe he was an engineer. He could have been in charge of various operational areas. Heck, he may have once been the cook. But now that he's the captain – should he be spending his time in the kitchen preparing dinner for the crew? Should he be creating navigational plans for their journey? Is he going to be in the engine room performing routine maintenance or repairs? He has a crew, and he delegates those tasks to them. Failing to do so could be disastrous for him, his crew, and the ship itself.

By not delegating, you'll find yourself running ragged to take care of tasks that should be handled by someone else on your team, all while hindering your ability to focus on higher-level strategic needs. You can't know if the ship is headed in the right direction if you're in the kitchen peeling potatoes.

If you're in a position of leadership, that means you have a team to lead. Whether that's 1 person (in addition to you) or 100, you won't get very far trying to do everything yourself. You have to delegate. Not only will effectively delegating help you accomplish everything that needs to get done, but your team members will feel trusted and empowered to take ownership over their work areas.

DIVIDE AND CONQUER

Whether delegation is a new concept for you or you're looking to enhance your delegation skills, let's explore several areas where you can get started:

- **Start small:** If this is new for you, begin with small, low-risk tasks that align with your team member's skills and abilities, to help build trust and confidence.
- **Clearly define expectations:** Communicate the objectives and expectations, as well as the desired

outcomes with your team members. Provide sufficiently detailed instructions with timelines and metrics for success if necessary.

- **Encourage ownership:** Empower your team members to complete their assigned tasks, encouraging them to independently make decisions as appropriate.

- **Provide support and resources:** Make sure your team has what they need in the form of resources, training, and tools to accomplish their assigned tasks and projects. Proactively offer guidance and support for any questions or challenges that may arise.

- **Establish clear communication channels:** Maintain open lines of communication with your team so they know they can come to you for input or advice. Create regular check-ins to ensure alignment and to address any issues that come up.

- **Celebrate success, learn from failure:** Publicly recognize the achievements of individual team members when they successfully complete tasks. When failures happen (when, not if), set the tone to show that these are learning opportunities to support a culture of continuous improvement.

- **Lead by example:** I still sometimes struggle with this one, and, as a result, deal with the pitfalls listed earlier in the chapter. If there are tasks that you're still doing that are a better fit for someone else, make the change.

- **Evaluate and adjust:** This is twofold: First, you might need to adjust plans, reassign tasks, or shift projects to different team members when priorities change or staffing levels decrease. This also applies to your own delegation practices – be open to feedback from your team and be willing to adapt your approach to best support them.

One tech-specific note about delegation – all I.T. teams need some sort of ticketing solution. This system will serve as a vital tool to efficiently manage tasks and requests, as well as improve communication and accountability in your organization. Additionally, a ticketing system provides great insights into your workload distribution, resource allocation, and team performance. You can prioritize your tasks based on urgency and impact, identify problem areas (or users), and create a standard/systemic approach to handling routine tasks. There are many free or low-cost ticketing solutions out there (because the lack of a ticketing system is not a technology problem, it's a **process** problem).

A DELICATE BALANCE

Despite the pitfalls associated with not delegating, there are also risks that come with over-delegating. Allow me to explain – imagine a team of four (including the manager) who are absolutely swamped with a major issue, an "all hands on deck" type of situation. The three staff members under the manager's oversight are running around, doing their best to put out technical fires. Meanwhile, the manager is sitting in their office, taking care of routine tasks. In this situation, it's far more important for the manager to roll up their sleeves and jump in to help the team. Remember – as a leader, your role is to lead and support your team. Sitting on the sidelines "delegating" when you could be chipping in during difficult times is not supporting your team.

There is no formula for how and when a leader should be "hands-on." Variables such as team size, complexity of the environment, number of offices, team member skillsets, and even organizational culture will influence this. Being able to discern when and how to jump in, and when to delegate and empower your team members to do what they do best, is a learnable skill. There is no one-size-fits-all approach, so consider factors like your team size, the complexity of the environment, the geographic locations of the office(s) you're supporting, and your team members' abilities when learning how to balance delegating and being hands-on.

Effective delegation is another foundational pillar of successful I.T. leadership. When properly utilized, you can unlock greater productivity, innovation, and overall success for yourself and your team. While some may hesitate to delegate tasks or projects, doing so is essential for fostering growth and preventing burnout. You'll unlock the full potential in both you and your team when you begin properly delegating!

In the next chapter, we'll dive into the third foundational pillar of leadership – strategy. An effective leader should be thinking strategically and proactively in support of their organization, and we'll explore how you can either begin doing so, or even expand your current strategic approach.

Key Takeaways:

- **It's essential:** Delegation is essential for effective leadership. Failure to delegate will result in decreased productivity, stifled innovation, and lower morale for your team.

- **Benefits of delegation:** Those who have mastered the skill of delegation find themselves more productive, more organized, and able to think strategically since they are not constantly in the trenches.
- **Overcoming hesitation:** Some hesitate to delegate, whether due to imposter syndrome, lack of trust, or other reasons. However, these reasons are never sufficient to avoid delegation.
- **Successful delegation:** By communicating effectively, setting clear goals, making yourself available, and starting small, you can begin to delegate successfully to your team.
- **Finding balance:** While it's possible to over-delegate, it is up to you to find the right balance.

Chapter 5:
Strategy

I was involved in a mentoring program that paired I.T. leaders with technology students from a local community college. This program involved group meetings and one-on-one coaching sessions. After the formal program ended, my mentee (*Evan*) and I decided to keep in touch, exchanging numbers and emails. Recently, he completed his degree in Information Systems and was hired to work in an entry-level role in I.T. support. I had helped him write his resume and offered advice on preparing for the interview, and he was thrilled to land the job! He was now the second person in a two-person team, providing support to an office of about 50 users spread across three regional offices.

While at a local coffee shop, we ran into each other and decided to sit and catch up for a few minutes. I was excited to hear how things were going in his new role.

"Busy," he laughed, taking a sip of his drink.

"Really?" I inquired. "I thought you would get bored quickly there since it's such a small place."

"We constantly seem to be putting out fires. It feels like every day, another server or service goes down, or someone's computer crashes. We just can't keep up with the workload. Our biggest issue is the email server. That thing constantly goes down. People aren't getting emails, or they can't connect to the server, or sometimes the backup job fails…it's such a pain.

"And I know what you're going to say," he laughed. "My manager doesn't want to outsource our email system. He says, and I quote, 'I don't have time to look into that'. I've tried to tell him how much easier our lives would be if we outsourced it to Microsoft or something, but he says he's too busy."

After hearing more about his challenges, I was intrigued and wanted to help. I asked him to create a "day in the life" document and send it to me. This way, we could review it together and look for some opportunities for improvement. We said our goodbyes and went about our days.

The following week, as I was wrapping up my day, my phone buzzed. I took it out and saw an email from him with the subject "day in the life". The email was very long – he might have used writing it out as a form of therapy to get it all off his chest. Here's a few highlights from Evan's "day in the life" as an I.T. helpdesk technician:

- Arrive in the office at 8am to find seven helpdesk emails sent from staff overnight or early in the morning. Several are complaining about their email not connecting. One had the infamous "blue screen of death", and another has a message on their Microsoft Word program that says the license is expired. I make calls and help out each user.

- Hear from Alex (*Evan's boss*) about how slammed they are and how busy he always is.

- Go into the server room and take the hard drives used for manual backups, starting the next job (I wish we could automate this or put it in the cloud!).

- Spend my morning putting out various fires from the previous evening, as well as new ones popping up. One user (Brenda) is upset because her computer is seven years old and too slow. She complains that she's been promised a new computer for years now, but there is no plan to replace it. I share her complaints with Alex, who says he'll get to it eventually.

- Go to lunch. Get called back from lunch while ordering food due to the email server failing for all users. Work with Alex to reboot the server and restart the email service. Eat vending machine snacks for lunch instead.
- Attend our weekly all-hands meeting. Hear from the CEO about a conference he attended, where he learned how other organizations were improving their processes by using Microsoft Teams. The CEO asks Alex about it, who tells them "It's on my radar, but I'll need to wrap up some projects first". Cry internally knowing he won't ever get to it.
- Have an existential crisis about my career choice.
- Work on documentation for our email server, in an effort to help Alex remember how to fix common or recurring issues. Sent a draft to Alex, who immediately responded that he would get to it when he had time.
- Check LinkedIn for new jobs (*kidding, sort of...*)

The poor guy was doing his best, but he kept hitting brick wall after brick wall in his efforts to make meaningful changes. Alex, his boss, failed to lead in any strategic way, leaving the organization to struggle with constant issues and inefficiencies. Without a proactive plan, they were stuck in a perpetual cycle of reactive problem-solving. I advised my friend and mentee that if Alex wasn't willing to change and couldn't think strategically, his best bet would be to polish up his resume and start looking for opportunities elsewhere. It was clear that unless Alex shifted his leadership to think more strategically, his current role would only continue to be a source of frustration.

THE FALSE DICHOTOMY

To successfully lead, a leader must, well, lead (shocking, I know, but stay with me). They must be able to break out of the day-to-day operations and focus on higher-level strategic plans and needs. This shift in perspective would allow them to guide their team to meet long-term goals rather than becoming overwhelmed with immediate tasks. In my experience working with leaders over the years, I've noticed that they tend to fall into one of two mindsets when it comes to strategic planning: **reactive** or **proactive**. Of course, both proactive and reactive approaches are necessary at different times, but the distinction between these two approaches (both *how*, and in the case of Alex, *when*) can make all the difference in the world.

A **reactive** leader is someone like Alex. This type of leader tends to make decisions and take actions only in response to issues or problems as they come up. As a result, they are often caught in a constant state of urgency, always responding to immediate crises, fires, or demands. This reactive approach creates an environment of inefficiency, increased stress, and missed opportunities for proactive improvement and growth. Someone like Alex (or those working with Alex) are likely to eventually find themselves in a state of burnout, perpetually stuck in crisis mode, without having many moments to breathe. Their focus is limited to the immediate needs, preventing them from seeing beyond to future challenges (or opportunities).

For non-technical leaders overseeing an I.T. department, managing a reactive I.T. leader can be particularly challenging. They regularly hear about how overworked and stressed their I.T. director is, how they need more help, more time, more staff. However, they may not be able to recognize that much of this stress in their I.T. department is self-inflicted due to a reactive approach.

On the flip side, a **proactive** leader is someone who anticipates challenges and opportunities, creating plans to address them before they arise. These leaders have a forward-thinking mindset, actively looking out for future risks and developing strategies to manage them effectively. This approach enables leaders and their teams to stay ahead of issues, minimize the impact of outages, and can identify and leverage new opportunities for efficiency and innovation.

Looking back at Evan's story through the lens of strategic proactive leadership, Alex (Evan's boss) would find some time to take a step back and see how much time and money they could save by outsourcing their aging, locally hosted email service to a cloud provider. This would free him up to look at other areas of inefficiency, such as replacing Brenda's old computer. Better yet, he could create a cyclical replacement plan to ensure all users will have the right equipment to support their needs. Alex could stabilize his department, reduce stress (both for himself, my mentee Evan, and end users like Brenda), and be freed up to look for new ways to support his company.

Most leaders tend to waver between proactive and reactive thinking, and I think that's a good thing. I know I just spent the last few paragraphs talking about the importance of a proactive approach – and it definitely is necessary from a strategic standpoint. But an effective leader needs to be able to walk a line between being proactive and reactive – thinking strategically how to best serve their organization, while also being ready to respond to immediate issues that can (and will) pop up at any time. For someone transitioning from a reactive stance to a proactive one, it often will be a gradual change. As time goes on and the department stabilizes, they will find more opportunities to think proactively.

It's important not to lean too heavily towards the proactive side either. While we definitely shouldn't be operating like Alex, constantly reactive, we must also avoid swinging the pendulum too far in the other direction. I've worked with organizations that overemphasize "strategy" and "governance", focusing almost entirely on proactive "planning". This is especially common in government agencies, where leaders often spend significant time planning projects, developing governance models, setting milestones, and defining success metrics – without actually making progress in their endeavors.

Additionally, the nature of the position itself may inherently lean more toward proactive or reactive approaches. For example, a Tier 1 helpdesk technician primarily responds to incoming tickets and service requests, operating in a reactive role. However, they can still be proactive by identifying trends in these requests and suggesting improvements to management to prevent recurring issues. There are also roles that require a balance of proactive and reactive approaches – such as I.T. Security. Professionals in this field **proactively** identify and address risks to their environment, while being prepared to **react** to security breaches or issues as they arise.

Effective leaders are able to avoid the false dichotomy of solely embracing either proactive or reactive approaches. They understand that in order to be successful in their role, they must be able to seamlessly ebb and flow between the two. One moment they are proactively writing a budget plan for the next fiscal year, and the next they are in reactive mode, addressing a major system failure. Thinking strategically, they take the initiative to address future challenges, opportunities, or goals. Their forward-thinking mindset allows them to anticipate challenges before they arise, seize opportunities as they present themselves, and fulfill their department and wider organizational goals. Simultaneously, they remain agile and responsive to rapidly evolving situations, stepping in to tackle immediate or urgent issues as they come up. When the emergency is over, they are supportive of their team members by continuously strategizing on how to prevent similar challenges in the future.

BREAKING IT DOWN

Strategic planning is a foundational pillar for success in any leadership role. It not only provides a roadmap for achieving organizational goals but also ensures that resources (human and financial) are being allocated effectively. Through deliberate planning, I.T. leaders empower themselves and their teams to enhance productivity, drive innovation, and consistently achieve their objectives. Drawing from our analogy in chapter 4 about a ship captain – they must strategically plan out where they want to go, plot their course, and consider potential risks they may face along the way. Even explorers with no official destination in mind had specific strategic goals to discover new lands, secure resources, or even circumvent the globe!

When planning for your organization, it's essential to break down your goals from high-level objectives into more specific plans. This process involves three distinct but interconnected areas of planning – **strategic**, **tactical**, and **transactional**:

- **Strategic:** Strategic planning involves defining overarching goals for your organization – in collaboration with other leaders – to align objectives, priorities, and requirements. These strategic goals serve as the foundation for the upcoming projects and initiatives. Larger organizations often develop comprehensive strategic plans for technology, with such goals as "Advancing I.T. Security", "Streamlining our I.T. Services" or "Increasing our Digital Presence to our Customers". These goals may be internally focused, aimed at improving operations, or externally focused to enhance customer experience or satisfaction.

- **Tactical:** Tactical planning focuses on the specific projects that will accomplish your organization's objectives or vision. This is where the strategic goals are translated into actionable technology projects. There is a close alignment or even overlap between strategic and tactical planning, often occurring simultaneously (depending on an organization's size). For instance, if a strategic goal is to "Streamline I.T. Services", a tactical project could involve digitizing outdated paper forms into electronic format.

- **Transactional:** Transactional planning includes the essential, day-to-day tasks required to support your organization's ongoing operations. In other words, this is the "boots on the ground" planning. This includes managing resources (human and financial), as well as adapting to any changes in these needs (temporary or permanent) resulting from new projects, initiatives, or goals.

As mentioned earlier, while strategic planning is crucial, it's equally important to avoid becoming overly engrossed in a cycle of planning without execution. These plans must be presented to leadership in a way that engages and excites them about the direction of your department. However, the process of crafting and presenting these plans can sometimes become overly bureaucratic or cumbersome. It's essential to tailor your planning approach to fit your organization's governance structure, ensuring that your goals are communicated clearly and in a digestible manger that avoids unnecessary procedural complexities.

WHERE TO BEGIN

Whether you're a new leader just getting started, an aspiring I.T. manager, or a seasoned director who that wants to be a more effective strategic planner, here are some first steps you can take today to begin to operate from a strategic standpoint:

- **Assess your current state:** Take a look at your current operations, systems, and processes. Ask questions like "Where are we now?", "What's working?", or, just as important, "What's not working?".

- **Create Goals and Objectives:** Considering the three areas of planning above, this is where you create your goals. What do you want to accomplish? How long will it take to accomplish it? How much will it cost? Consider following a framework such as SMART goals (Specific, Measurable, Achievable, Relevant, and Time-bound).

- **Plan Collaboratively:** Be intentional to involve key stakeholders and team members in your planning process. Hold workshops or meetings to share your goals and objectives and be open to the perspectives and opinions from various departments.

- **Evaluate your market:** Stay informed about industry trends and market developments. What emerging technologies can support our goals? Is there something new that can give your organization a competitive edge? Are you using it, and if not, why? (because your competitor probably will!)

- **Consider risks:** Conduct risk assessments to identify potential obstacles and uncertainties. Ask questions such as "what would happen if we don't do this?" or "what would happen if this project failed?" Create mitigation plans to safeguard from these risks.

- **Communicate and collaborate:** Foster an environment of open communication and collaboration across departments and teams. Keep stakeholders informed about your planning process, objectives, and progress. Encourage feedback and incorporate diverse perspectives into strategic decision-making to ensure comprehensive alignment and engagement.

- **Establish Metrics and track progress:** Define key performance indicators (KPIs) and metrics to measure progress. For example, if you're transitioning from paper to digital forms, a goal could be to decrease processing time. Regularly monitor and adjust your approach based on performance to stay on track.

ROAD TRIP

I like to think of strategic planning like preparing to take a vacation. First, you proactively decide on the destination (where do you want to go?). You also plan ahead by scheduling time off work, arranging for a pet sitter, and budgeting for the costs – much like setting goals and objectives for your organization.

Next, you take the time to decide what car you will take, map out the route, and pack your essentials to bring with you. This is like tactical planning, where you're determining the specific actions and projects needed to achieve your strategic goals. Finally, there's the transactional needs – the day-to-day logistics of driving, navigating, and managing pit stops.

Despite your thorough planning, unexpected challenges will probably happen – a flat tire, road closures, or inclement weather – forcing you to into reactive mode. However, because you've already mapped out your destination, you can adapt and overcome these obstacles, staying focused on reaching your goal of making it to the beautiful beach house you rented for the weekend!

To plan is to be intentional. Sure, with our road trip example – maybe you could just get in the car and drive, seeing where the road takes you. That works on vacation (usually), but it doesn't work in business leadership. Effective leadership requires a proactive approach, breaking free from the day-to-day and thinking outside the box. You must also be ready to react quickly to unexpected challenges while maintaining your proactive mindset.

By combining strategic, tactical, and transactional planning, you will maximize your potential and set you and your organization up for success!

Key Takeaways:

- **It's essential:** Strategic planning is another essential pillar for effective leadership.
- **Proactive vs. reactive:** Leaders typically fall into either proactive or reactive approaches, but a good leader must lean more into proactive planning for

success, while being ready to transition quickly into reactive mode.

- **Balanced approach:** A good leader can balance proactive and reactive approaches according to their organization's unique size, structure, and needs.
- **Don't forget to work:** Overemphasis on proactive planning can impede your ability to get work done.
- **Integrated planning:** By integrating **strategic**, **tactical**, and **transactional** planning, you'll be positioned to lead your team to success.

Richard Blalock

PART III:
THE PEOPLE

While technology might serve as the foundation for an I.T. department, it is the **people** who bring it to life. The next three chapters emphasize the human element of leadership, focusing on managing and empowering your team to be successful.

Effective recruiting is the first step to building a strong team. We need the best people who not only have the required skills but also align with your organization's culture and values. Once they are onboard, creating and maintaining a healthy work culture is essential. A positive, supportive environment enhances employee satisfaction, retention, and overall productivity. Of course, disagreements and conflict are inevitable, so we'll explore how to handle them effectively – turning potential obstacles into opportunities for growth and improvement.

By refining your people management skills, you'll not only build a more cohesive and motivated team but also elevate your organization to new levels of success. Let's look at how to develop a thriving team – the true backbone of I.T. success.

Chapter 6:
The Talent is Out There

I recently attended a technology conference focused on the latest advancements in the public sector. It was great reconnecting with old colleagues and friends after the event had been cancelled for a few years due to the COVID-19 pandemic. After a long day of attending presentations, breakout sessions, and exploring the massive vendor exhibit hall, I joined my friends (we'll call them Emily and Jacob) for a much-needed happy hour. As we settled in with our drinks, our conversation turned to the topic of recruiting for I.T. positions.

"So, how's the hiring process going for your I.T. security position?" Emily asked Jacob.

"Bad," he sighed, frustration evident in his voice. "We've had very few qualified applicants. Many of them are asking for salaries beyond our budget, while others insist on telecommuting or flexible work hours. It's been rough, and don't even get me started on the flood of applications from security guards!"

"Can't you offer some of these flexible options?" Emily inquired.

"Nope, that's not really how we work in my unit." Jacob shrugged. "I like seeing everyone each day in person. We work better as a team in person, kicking things off with our daily standup. We typically all get in at the same time and leave at the same time."

He took another sip, before continuing. "We'll find someone eventually, a warm body to fill the role. Say, what about you Emily? Didn't you recruit for a security analyst earlier this year?"

"I did! It was a lot of work to find the right person. We had nearly 100 applicants!" Emily replied, her tone upbeat and confident.

Jacob nearly choked on his drink. "100! Shoot, send some of them my way! What's your secret?"

"Well," Emily began, "With this job, we knew that it could be done from anywhere, so we opted to try out telecommuting. I think that's a big reason why. We also heavily promoted the job on LinkedIn and other social networks, as well as a ton of online job search platforms. We did, of course, have our share of security guard candidates, but overall, we had a large pool to choose from. It took forever for us to go through the resumes, and we interviewed the top 10 before making an offer. Our new gal is great, she's been with us for a few months now!"

As we wrapped up our dinner and drinks and headed to our individual rooms, bracing for another day of the event, I couldn't shake off the glaring disparities in Jacob and Emily's recruitment approaches. Jacob's insistence on mandating their I.T. Security Analyst work solely in their office (in a city notorious for its high cost-of-living) was drastically limiting his applicant pool. I also couldn't help but remember Jacob's reference to a "warm body", which stood in contrast to Emily's proactive and inclusive recruitment strategy.

WHERE ARE WE GOING?

I mentioned before how I've sat on various hiring panels to select new I.T. staff – both in my career as well as in various consulting engagements. In the context of the consulting role, the engagement often begins with a panicked call from a company executive. They tell us how their long-term I.T.

person is retiring after a long career, and nobody really knows what exactly it is they do. The request is typically for us to help them find someone to replace their longstanding employee and keep things running smoothly.

However, I always tell my clients that before hiring a replacement, it's important to first consider what you actually need in the role. Having a long-term staff member retire or leave their position is a great opportunity to reevaluate your needs that were being met by that role. If you were struggling to get effective support from the previous person, it's probably not a good idea to just dust off their job description from 10 years ago and post it on job boards. Check in with your other staff to see what was working and, just as importantly, what wasn't working.

Some specific questions to ask when hiring:

- Were you satisfied with the level of support you were getting?
- Were you happy with how they communicated their status to you (or other leadership)?
- Is your organization pivoting in a different direction or making strategic changes, and if so, how will that impact the I.T. department?

- Do you have any major projects on the horizon, and how will I.T. be involved in them?

- Do you have any *technology-specific* projects coming up, and if so, what skills would ensure the project's success?

- Has there been an increased demand for I.T. services in a certain area which requires a specific skill set?

In other words, you have to know where you are going and what you need before hiring the person to take you there.

While these guidelines typically apply to replacing a team member, the logic also applies when expanding your team by hiring a new staff member. In this situation, you should know already what projects, tasks and assignments the new staff will have.

UNDERSTANDING YOUR ORGANIZATION

When hiring for I.T. positions, you need to look beyond simply hiring a "tech" who can fix the computer, get the printer to print, reboot the server, or back up the network. There are millions of people out there that can do that. But that's not enough anymore. It's no longer sufficient to just find a warm body that can "fix it". In the past, I.T. was often viewed as a mysterious department tucked away in the basement (why the basement, I'm not sure). They performed seemingly magical tasks to keep the technology running smoothly. But it's a new day.

Many I.T. staff have impressive resumes demonstrating the right education, experience, and certifications that can show, on paper at least, that they are qualified to do the job you're hiring for. They can give you a laundry list of certifications, applications they are familiar with, how many workstations they supported in their previous role, past migration projects completed, tickets resolved, or any other metric that demonstrates they can do the work. While these are all important indicators of their capabilities, they only scratch the surface. It's important to dig deeper beyond the credentials and experience to properly assess their suitability for the role.

I had a friend who used to work as a courtroom clerk, docketing the activities and actions taken in a high-paced, busy courtroom. Some courtroom calendars had over 100 people scheduled to appear. One day the judge's computer – used to view the defendant's record, charges, and other critical information – stopped working. The judge was unable to proceed with the court calendar without it, so he paused proceedings and asked my friend to call I.T. for help. She promptly phoned down to the technical services department to report the problem (which was causing everything to screech to a halt in the courtroom). After sharing the issues with the tech, his reply was blunt: "Did you put in a ticket yet?".

In this story, I would bet that Mr. Grumpy Tech had the certifications, degrees, and/or experience required to do his job. But he was not able to grasp the operational impact that the technical failure had on his organization.

When scouting for I.T. talent, you're not just searching for any run-of-the-mill tech. You need someone who can learn and understand your specific business needs and then apply the right technology to support them. In my court example, it didn't matter whether or not my friend had "put in a ticket." What mattered most was that Mr. Grumpy Tech hustled into that courtroom and resolve the issue, stat.

Knowing what your needs are will influence what you write in your job posting. It's crucial to be as thorough and descriptive as possible, outlining the job duties, requirements, and responsibilities clearly both in the description and during the interview (more on interviews shortly). It wastes everyone's time if you are not clear about the details of the role and end up having candidates (or worse, new hires!) drop out.

Several years ago, I accepted a new job at another organization, and put in my notice with my current employer, where I had worked for seven years. I agreed to help them train my replacement. I was proud of the progress I had made as a single-person I.T. department and wanted to ensure they kept the momentum going with the next person. The role had evolved over the years since I had first started, which included some accounting-related tasks that weren't difficult in nature but were assigned to me out of necessity due to the computer system in use at the time.

However, the job posting didn't reflect the new tasks, and I wasn't included in the interview panel. Eventually, I was contacted by my old employer with the good news – they had hired someone new! I scheduled time to meet with him for a few days of hands-on training (thankful to my new employer at the time for being flexible with this).

On the third day, we were working through the detailed accounting tasks. I noticed that my replacement (*Dave*) was confused. "This wasn't on the job description", he said, scratching his beard.

"I know, but this needs to be done by us due to the finicky-ness of the system. It's not complicated. Here, take a look", I showed him the documentation I had drafted outlining the steps to take to complete the task.

"I'm an I.T. guy, I'm not an accountant. I didn't sign up for this." Dave stood up, and – I kid you not – walked out of the room, quitting on the spot. Bewildered, I called my old boss to tell her the news. This was the only candidate that passed their evaluations and interviews. Ultimately, they were forced to re-post the job – this time with an updated list of duties to include the accounting responsibilities – and were able to find another person to fill the role.

All of this trouble – months of wasted time – could have been avoided had my old employer taken the time to evaluate their needs and make sure the job description was updated. It's worth the effort to make sure your job posting includes all the relevant responsibilities that are expected of the role. This extra step will save you from potential future headaches.

BOOSTING YOUR APPLICANT POOL

Now that we've identified our needs and ensured they're accurately reflected in the job posting, let's avoid the predicament that Jacob faced at the beginning of the chapter – struggling to find a single qualified candidate. Before releasing your job posting into the wild, consider a few other factors that could boost the number of applicants:

- **Salary:** This is the first and most obvious item to consider – ensure your salary is competitive. While we all want to maximize value for our organization, it's important to recognize that I.T. salaries are typically higher than in other fields. Research fair salaries for the role by comparing them with similar postings and be sure to account for regional variations. Additionally, factor in bonuses, stock options, or other financial incentives.

- **Remote or telework opportunities:** The demand for remote work continues to rise, especially after the lockdowns associated with the COVID-19 pandemic. Evaluate (or reconsider) whether this position allows for remote work, considering the job requirements and team dynamics. Be explicit in both the posting and interview about any details (such as the number of days per week allowed). For instance, implementing a rotating telework schedule for helpdesk staff can offer flexibility without compromising productivity.

- **Flexible hours and scheduling:** Similarly, offering flexible scheduling can attract applicants who are seeking a better work-life balance. Tailor this option to the position requirements and organizational needs.

- **Work-life balance:** Candidates are increasingly prioritizing employers known for fostering a healthy work-life balance. Evaluate (or reconsider) your approach to scheduling, identify any crunch times with additional workload, and be sure to share your organization's overall stance in this area.

- **Promotional opportunities:** This applies to both the job posting and the interview. Highlighting opportunities for growth within your organization can help attract applicants. Consider outlining pathways for growth – such as training programs, mentorship opportunities, or leadership tracks.

A note on telework and flexible hours: these options are great for the right people who can bring their talents and experience to benefit your organization. However, some of these benefits could be taken advantage of. For example, if you offer telecommuting, more flexible hours, and promote a culture of work/life balance, it's possible (maybe even inevitable) for a staff member to abuse these benefits by showing up late, leaving early, being ineffective with their tasks, or just blowing off work for the day. This is a tangible risk associated with these benefits. However, with the right leadership skills (which we talked about in chapters 3-5) and the right culture (which we will explore in chapter 7), I find that these people reveal themselves, and should be addressed accordingly. As a leader, it's essential to maintain high standards while offering high rewards. If someone abuses the benefits you offer, then they are not a good fit for your organization and should be dealt with swiftly.

THE INTERVIEW

Now that we've identified our needs, updated the position description, and posted the job, it's time to interview! By this point, if you're calling someone for an interview, it means that they have demonstrated, at least on paper, that they meet the qualifications for the position and have the right level of experience.

The interview should serve two purposes: First, it's to verify and validate that the person has the skills and experience they said they did in their application. For this, you should include some questions that prompt the candidate to expand and elaborate on their experiences and technical abilities. Second, the interview is also your chance to evaluate other areas for your candidates – such as cultural fit, communication style, and the ability to operate under pressure. Here are a few things to consider when interviewing:

- **Reviewing the resume:** Take a few moments before the interview to refresh your memory on the candidate's education, experience, and other details. The cover letter can also provide insights into their written communication skills.

- **Dress code:** Call me old-fashioned, but I believe that if you're showing up for an interview, you should dress your best. COVID caused many interviews to become Zoom meetings, and that's only exacerbated the issue. It's not a good look when the hiring panel is better dressed than the candidate. Even if your organization has a more relaxed environment (or even a uniform), it's reasonable to expect the candidate you're interviewing to be dressed up.

- **Communication skills:** Assess their ability to communicate effectively, especially if the role involves directly supporting end users, or will be expected to give presentations to other staff. Look for clarity, simplicity, and adaptability in their communication style, and watch out for that overly technical jargon.
- **Problem solving:** I.T. professionals don't have all the answers, but they should demonstrate a willingness to find solutions. Pay attention to how they approach unfamiliar questions or scenarios.
- **Integrating with business needs:** The interview is a good opportunity to see what, if anything, the candidate knows about your organization. It's reasonable to expect a candidate to have done some research into your company, so asking a question along the lines of "what do you know about (*company*)?" can reveal that. Their ability to respond positively to this question is also directly related to their ability to avoid acting like Mr. Grumpy Tech I shared about earlier in the chapter.
- **Cultural Fit:** This is an important, but often overlooked, area. This person will be spending 40 hours a week (maybe more) working for your

organization. I encourage people to expand the interview panel beyond just the candidate's potential supervisor, manager, or director. Including a colleague at the same level can help show whether the candidate will fit in with the team. The colleague could ask more fun/casual questions such as "what are your hobbies?" to create a more relaxed atmosphere for discussing personal interests and work preferences.

WELCOME ABOARD

After completing the interviews, you've found an outstanding candidate! With their impressive experience, strong communication skills, and clear understanding of your organization, they are a perfect fit. You even brought them back for a second interview and a meet-and greet with your team, who all found them to be pleasant to talk to. Congratulations! It's time to make an offer! By following the steps outlined in this chapter, you're not just filling a position – you're setting up a successful and rewarding partnership.

But hiring someone is the first step in the journey. Once they're in the door (or online, if telecommuting!), how are you supporting them to be successful? In the next chapter, we will discuss the importance of creating and maintaining a positive and healthy workplace culture and provide actionable strategies to cultivate such an environment within your organization.

Key takeaways:

- **Understand organizational needs:** Before hiring someone, you must first understand where your organization is going and whether the previous person in the role fully met your needs. Hiring new staff is a great opportunity to first reassess and realign the job requirements with your current and future goals.

- **Beyond technical skills:** It is no longer enough to hire someone with the right technical skills. They must also demonstrate an understanding of your organization's unique needs and apply the right technology to support them.

- **Boosting applicant pool:** Factors such as salary, benefits, flexible work options, and work-life balance can significantly boost your applicant pool. Highlighting promotional opportunities within your organization can also attract ambitious candidates looking for career growth.

- **Reconsider Telework:** Telework should be reconsidered for nearly all I.T. positions. While it offers flexibility and can expand your applicant pool, be vigilant about those who might take advantage of the offer. Implement measures to ensure accountability and productivity.

- **Effective Interviewing:** The interview is your opportunity to verify that candidates can perform the required duties and to determine if they are a good fit for your organization. Assess their communication skills, problem-solving abilities, cultural fit, and understanding of your business needs.

Chapter 7:
Building the Culture

A few years back, my company was contacted to perform an I.T. security assessment for a law firm. These engagements were fairly straightforward: audit the firm's systems and networks, identify any potential risks, and help them address those risks. We also met with end users to quiz them on their knowledge of the company's policies and ensure they followed them (this is where we would catch staff writing their passwords on sticky notes attached to their monitors!).

This wasn't something I typically participated in, but we were short one team member who was on extended leave, so I agreed to pitch in and help out. I would perform the end-user interviews and talk with the technical team to learn who handled the I.T. security tasks (and how they were managed). Before arriving, we learned that the I.T. director – a man who had been in the role for over 20 years – had just retired. They did not appoint someone internally to fill the role on an interim basis, so the position was sitting vacant.

At the end of our onsite kickoff meeting with the I.T. team, I had to ask. "The last director was here for over 20 years and just left a month ago. That's a long time to work in a job like that. How did you all like working under (*Bill*)?"

There was an uncomfortable long pause, with awkward chair shifting and glances around the room.

"…that bad, huh?" I chuckled.

We spent the next 30 minutes discussing Bill, and it quickly became clear that he was far from a good boss. Their stories revealed a man who was infamous for his micromanagement and a heavy-handed, authoritarian style. In group meetings, he was known to publicly criticize individual team members for the most trivial of reasons. One team member recounted an incident where they were written up for arriving a mere two minutes late, despite an excellent attendance record and calling the director beforehand to inform him that his car was having issues. Another shared a memo issued a few years back, threatening to dock vacation time for any bathroom breaks that Bill deemed "extensive." Finally, we all got a chuckle out of Bill's "training session" which "taught" staff to prioritize email recipients by seniority and insisted on using a specific font and size in email messages.

As they continued to share, I felt a wave of empathy wash over me. These poor folks had been subject to an extremely unhealthy work culture, and it all stemmed from the director. It was obvious they were glad Bill was gone, but I could also sense a tension of uncertainty in the air related to the new, yet-to-be-hired boss. Would they be the same? What if they were worse?

I left the meeting with the belief that our engagement with the law firm needed to expand. In a meeting later that day with the Vice President of Operations (*Jennifer*), I brought up Bill's retirement and asked how their job search was going.

"I see Bill left about a month ago. How's the job search going?"

Jennifer frowned. "Not good. We have a few decent applicants, but we were really hoping that someone already on the team would apply. Nobody did."

Seizing the opportunity, I asked, "How did you enjoy working with Bill?"

"He was fine, I guess," she stammered before continuing: "I don't really know much about I.T., and he had already been here for so long, he seemed like he really knew what he was doing, so I just let it be."

"Did you ever meet with him to learn his projects? What about his staff?"

"It was weird. Bill would insist in leadership meetings that if anyone wanted to talk with someone on his team, they first go through him. He told us that they were so busy that he needed to be the point person. So not really. In fact," she paused, taking a sip of her coffee. "I noticed that at any office party or event, which we make optional, Bill was never there, and members of his team rarely showed up either. I.T. was kind of their own little world. Anyways… how is the security review going? When can we expect to see the report?"

I cringed, concern obvious on my face. "I think we should keep talking about Bill."

After a long discussion, Jennifer agreed to expand the engagement to include a leadership support role. We were going to help them find a new captain for their ship. To start, it was important that Jennifer understood the full extent of the issues that had plagued the department. As a leader, she had failed to recognize some of the tell-tale signs of problems and needed to be caught up. It was also important that we empower her to be able to effectively support the new I.T. director and ensure that cultural challenges didn't creep back in.

Jennifer and I set up a "town hall" of sorts with the I.T. team members. To help make the environment more welcoming, we brought in some snacks and drinks (food always helps). We set the tone of the meeting as an open forum – we wanted to hear everything that they had experienced. No holding back, nobody would get in trouble for sharing how they really felt.

The team members were initially reserved, unsure what they should share. I broke the ice by asking about what I had heard earlier regarding the timing of bathroom breaks, which – by the look on her face – you could tell that Jennifer had not heard about. After that, the group opened up more, sharing (and venting) their experiences and frustrations. Jennifer simply listened, occasionally taking notes.

Once they were done, there was a brief pause before Jennifer spoke softly. "I'm sorry." Looking over at her, I could see a mixture of sadness and disappointment on her face as she continued. "I could try to shift the blame by saying I'm not technical, and that's why I didn't keep tabs on Bill as much as I should have.

"But none of these issues were technical. These were all, simply put, a failure of leadership – both for Bill, who frankly should have been fired years ago, but also on me. I can promise you that we will fix this."

I worked with them over the next several weeks, reviewing and updating the job description, and bolstering their announcement and description to strongly emphasize the need for a collaborative leader with a positive attitude. We met with the team to learn their projects and statuses, which helped inform the interview questions we created, and ultimately landed a new leader.

While the engagement was considered complete as far as my company was concerned, I did get a final email from Jennifer a few weeks later, thanking me for helping them out, and sharing how they held a "meet and greet" with the new Director. My client was starting out on the right foot, and I was confident they were in good hands going forward.

IT STARTS WITH YOU

The culture of an organization can be just as important in retaining staff as other factors like salary, benefits, hours, or promotional opportunities. I've seen people leave good-paying jobs for the same or even less pay due to a bad culture. When reviewing resumes, many candidates show work history in positions that lasted a short time. While some instances are due to people job hopping to move up or make more money, it's insightful to ask about their short tenures during interviews. While they may be vague, generic, or trying to be nice, you also end up with some interesting or outright wild stories of aggressive bosses, hostile work environments, office fights, teammates hiding when their boss is around, ghosting one another, office politics, and more.

As a leader, you are responsible for building a healthy culture in your organization. It doesn't matter if you're taking over a team of seasoned veterans who have been working their jobs for years. You're now in a position of authority to lead and guide this group of people – you can start by setting the tone to be more positive, encouraging, and supportive. You don't have to sacrifice your high standards of work to build this culture.

Below is a list of things you can start doing to set the tone with your team:

- **Praise in public:** Bill should have learned this long ago. Be intentional by highlighting recent project successes that a team member accomplished during team meetings. Acknowledge their achievements by including their ability to overcome challenges associated with the project.

- **Criticize in private:** Never, ever criticize an employee in any group or public setting. Take time to meet with them privately and address the problem succinctly, keeping a solution-oriented mindset. Be sure to incorporate how or why it's important that they address their mistakes. You can also maintain that positive tone in these discussions.

- **Dump the ego:** We make mistakes too (big shocker, I know). When this happens – own it. Don't deflect, don't blame another staff member, and don't try to justify the mistake. Remember, you set the tone and culture for your team. If you start deflecting responsibility, they will too. When you screw up, own the mistake, make a plan to fix it going forward, and follow through with that plan.

- **Make yourself available:** It's easy to get caught up in all the work you and your team have to do. Days fill up with various meetings, check-ins, standups, project updates, conferences, site visits, and work travel – you know how it goes. But you can never be too busy to make time to meet with your team. If they have a concern – whether it's about a work task, another employee, or even yourself – they should have an avenue to connect with you and discuss. An "open door policy" means just that – you're available, at any time (within reason), to connect with individual team members and hear them out. This doesn't mean you have to agree with everything they say (sometimes there isn't anything that can be done), but often just making yourself available to meet and hear them out is enough.

I mentioned earlier the topic of high standards. You should have the highest standards for yourself in the area of culture setting. By following the above practices, you'll be well on your way to instilling a positive culture in your environment.

TEAM INVESTMENT

One often overlooked area of culture setting is how well you're investing in the wellness of your own team members. As the old saying goes, "People don't care what you know until they know that you care." I'm a big fan of the American television series "The Office." In the show, the main character Michael Scott frequently references how his employees are "his best friends," and you often find him getting himself into funny but awkward situations to maintain his approach. By contrast, his predecessor, who makes a brief appearance in one episode, frustratingly asks Michael, "Why can't you let your workers be your workers, your family be your family, your friends be your friends?"

I think it's somewhere in the middle. You don't have to be best friends with your team members (in fact, I'd generally discourage it), but you also shouldn't maintain an uncomfortable degree of separation with everyone on your team either. Regardless of where you fall in this grey area, by investing in the well-being of your staff, you will produce happier, healthier, and more productive employees.

Here are some initial steps you can take as a leader to invest in your team:

- **Interests and hobbies:** Your staff aren't just a bunch of mindless zombies who only work. They have interests and hobbies outside of the job, just like you. This is an area you can set the tone – start by sharing what you did over the weekend, as you feel comfortable. This could lead to fun discussions about skiing experiences, swapping the best hiking trails in the area, the latest books they're reading, or even some friendly sports banter about your favorite NBA team. This is a great tangible step to build a more fun atmosphere and can also help team members let their guard down a bit.

- **How, not just what:** In my regular one-on-one meetings with team members, I like to begin by asking how they are doing, how their weekend was, and sharing anything relevant from my life. This may seem arbitrary, as the term "how's it going" is as commonplace as a simple hello, but I love to ask and listen. Through these questions, I get to know more about their families, friends, and interests. As time goes on and I get to know my team better, I can ask, "How did your son do with their (spelling bee, baseball game, band concert)?" On the other side of the coin, it helps to know if one of your team members is having a hard time with something outside of work and can influence a more empathetic approach to these situations. Some of your team members may not respond much to these requests. Perhaps they're naturally more private. That's fine; recognize and adjust. The whole point of this isn't to just check a box that you asked them how they're doing; it's to show that you care (because you should care).

- **Where are they going:** It's important to learn and understand the career aspirations of your individual team members. This may be obvious and come up naturally during regular discussions, hearing about their efforts in completing a degree or certification, or even if they ask to participate in tasks or projects that better align with their career interests. One of the best opportunities to learn this is through the performance review process – when you're reviewing their past accomplishments and challenges and setting goals for the future. Once you're aware of their goals, start looking for opportunities in your workplace that align with them. If your budget affords it, invest in training courses or – better yet – a subscription service that offers a catalog of courses (such as LinkedIn Learning or Pluralsight). Working with your staff, identify classes that support their career goals and interests, and encourage them to carve out some time to go through them. This can also help you as a leader in identifying promotional opportunities from within, and even help with succession planning for your own role.

One note on team investment: Some of this may not hit home as perfectly as I described it. Perhaps you're trying to get to know someone, but there's a wall there. That's OK. Some people may not reciprocate the relationship you're trying to build here, and you'll need to respect that. But the reality is that you're spending 40+ hours a week with these people, often in stressful or difficult situations. You might as well do your part to build an environment to be as enjoyable as possible.

ATTITUDE REFLECTS LEADERSHIP

Building a healthy, positive culture in the workforce begins with you. As a leader, you have a responsibility to create this environment within your own team – even if it's not present in other teams, offices, or divisions in your organization. The steps outlined in this chapter are not comprehensive by any means; there are many more strategies that can be pursued to improve morale in your team. But at the end of the day, it's an intentional decision that you must make. I can guarantee you that by doing so, you'll see great results in the form of happier and more productive employees. What do you have to lose?

A key aspect of maintaining a positive culture is effectively managing interpersonal conflict. In the next chapter, we'll outline strategies for handling conflict within your team, understanding its root causes, and turning potential friction points into opportunities for growth and collaboration. Conflict is inevitable, but with the right approach, it can be managed constructively.

Key Takeaways:

- **Prioritize Positive Culture:** The culture of an organization can be as crucial in retaining staff as the salary, benefits, and promotional opportunities. People often leave well-paying jobs due to negative work environments.
- **Leadership Responsibility:** As a leader, you are responsible for setting and maintaining the team culture. Whether you inherit a team or build one from scratch, you set the tone for a positive, encouraging, and supportive environment.
- **Get started:** While not comprehensive, some tangible strategies you can begin to take include praising in public, critiquing in private, owning your mistakes,

and making yourself available with an open-door policy.

- **Remember the how:** Show genuine care for your team's well-being. Understanding their interests, hobbies, and personal challenges can create a supportive atmosphere that enhances productivity and job satisfaction.
- **Career Growth Support:** Learn and support your team members' career aspirations. Providing opportunities for growth and development shows that you value their future and can improve retention and engagement.

Chapter 8:
On Conflict

It's a tale as old as time:

Sara is an experienced helpdesk team member, known for her meticulous attention to detail. She responds to tickets quickly and accurately, always providing thorough explanations for how she resolved each support request. While her professional and precise approach ensures issues are comprehensively addressed, end users often find her somewhat standoffish and unnecessarily detailed.

In the next cubicle sits her colleague, Joseph. Everyone loves Joseph. Outgoing, witty, and always the life of the party, you can usually find Joseph cutting it up in the break room with his colleagues. Joseph prides himself on completing the most tickets every month, and some end users specifically ask for him when calling or writing in for help. However, when other members of Joseph's team are asked to give him feedback, they'll admit that they don't like the lack of detail he provides in the ticketing system, which leads to more work for the next tech to untangle what he did.

One day, Sara approaches Joseph's cubicle and clears her throat.

Joseph spins around in his chair. "Hey! What's up, Sara?"

"I'm working on a ticket for Amber in accounting. Something about the accounts not batching in the finance software."

"Oh yeah, I remember that happened last month. Need help?"

"I don't need your help," Sara replies curtly. "I'm looking at the ticket you left here. There's nothing here I can work with to figure it out. What did you do to fix it?"

"Oh man, I can't remember. Tell you what, why don't you just reassign the ticket to me, and I'll take care of it."

"I told you, I don't need your help," Sara snaps. "If you did your job better, I'd be able to see how you fixed the error and could do it myself. You never put anything in the notes of your tickets!"

"Whoa, chill out, Sara," Joseph shoots back. "I don't want to hear any guff about my tickets. Everyone knows I complete the most on the team."

"Besides," he continues, spinning back around in his chair, "Amber told me in the break room that she wished I would be the one helping her out anyway. Maybe if you tried being a bit nicer."

"Well, we can't always be the life of the party. Some of us have work to do!"

Sara storms off in one direction, Joseph in the other.

IT'S INEVITABLE

Despite our best efforts as leaders, conflict is inevitable. It's part of human nature. Conflicts can arise from various sources such as simple miscommunications, misunderstandings, poor communication channels, or different personality styles. In the scenario above, we see how differing work styles and a lack of effective communication can lead to friction. Conflicts may also stem from competing goals or priorities, unclear roles and expectations, or personal stressors spilling into the workplace. Recognizing these sources and addressing them proactively is crucial for maintaining a harmonious and productive work environment.

As a leader, you must be prepared to navigate sources of conflict—whether it's between yourself and others, among members of your team, or even with your own superiors. Specifically, in the I.T. field, where many roles interact with all users in an organization, the chance of conflict is even higher. The nature of I.T. work often involves high stress, tight deadlines, and a constant demand for problem-solving, which can all contribute to conflicts.

By not intentionally working through conflict as it arises, you're opening up your team and your organization to a slew of challenges. These can include poor team dynamics, increased stress, missed opportunities for improvement, and higher turnover. Additionally, unresolved conflicts can prevent the advancement of talented staff, leading to frustration, disengagement, and eventual separation from the job. In more severe cases, persistent conflict can expose your organization to reputational or even legal concerns.

In this chapter, we'll explore ways to recognize the signs and symptoms of brewing conflict. We'll also discuss areas of conflict that are more common or unique in the I.T. field, such as issues arising from rapid technological changes, differing levels of technical expertise, and the high-pressure environment of I.T. support. We'll then dive into high-level strategies for conflict resolution, including effective communication, setting clear expectations, and fostering a collaborative environment. Lastly, we'll examine strategies to prevent future conflicts and highlight why some conflicts can be healthy. By understanding and managing conflict, you can turn these challenging situations into opportunities for growth and improvement.

RECOGNIZING THE SIGNS

It can be easy to miss or overlook brewing challenges with your staff. Perhaps you're neck-deep in a project and not paying close attention to what's going on in the office. Maybe you're in the middle of hiring new staff and focusing on filling the right roles (following the advice in Chapter 6, I'm sure!). Your team might be hybrid or fully remote, making it more difficult to recognize the signs of conflict. Or, perhaps you're conflict-avoidant, which is something you as a leader should work on (remembering the consequences of not dealing with conflict, as discussed earlier).

Here are some tell-tale signs that you may have ongoing conflict within your team:

- **Hostile Communication**: When asked a question, Frank's responses are suddenly oozing with sarcasm or passive-aggressiveness, when previously he was friendly and polite. This shift in tone can be a clear indicator of underlying frustration or resentment.

- **Avoidance**: You notice that Clint and Don are no longer speaking, either directly (despite their offices being next to each other) or indirectly during meetings. Avoidance can often signal unresolved issues and a desire to evade confrontation.

- **Blaming**: When confronted with a missed deadline, Susan lashes out and blames her colleagues, refusing to take responsibility. Blaming can create a toxic environment, undermining trust and collaboration.

- **Productivity Slump**: Amy's productivity has taken a noticeable slump – in both the quantity and quality of her work – despite a previous track record of high performance. Such changes can be linked to personal grievances, burnout, or demotivation due to unresolved conflict.

Recognizing these signs early is crucial for addressing conflicts before they escalate. As a leader, it's important to stay attuned to the dynamics within your team, even when other responsibilities demand your attention. This intentional focus enables you to intervene quickly and prevent situations from spiraling out of control.

I.T. SPECIFIC

In the field of I.T., where staff support every user in the organization, specific interpersonal challenges often arise. Here are some key areas to consider:

- **Within the Team:** Using our fictional story of Sara and Joseph as an example, we see a typical conflict that can frequently occur. Differences in work styles, approaches to solving problems, or even personality differences can contribute to tension within your team. It's essential to recognize these differences and address them proactively to maintain a cohesive working environment.

- **With End Users:** Since I.T. interacts with every part of an organization, conflicts with end users are common. These situations can include dissatisfaction with the level of service, a lack of communication about a problem, or passive-aggressive behavior from frustrated users. For instance, an end user may be difficult to work with, ignoring your instructions on resolving an issue. Handling these conflicts with patience and clear communication (which we learned about in chapter 4) is crucial to maintaining positive relationships and effective support.

- **With Management:** There's an old saying in I.T.: when everything is working perfectly, the boss will say, "What do I pay you for?" When something breaks, the boss will say, "What do I pay you for?" This sarcastic example highlights a common challenge in the I.T. field. As outlined in Chapter 5, effective communication with your leaders is crucial. They may not fully understand the technical details of the situations you're working through and might express frustration during outages or failures. Clear, regular communication and setting realistic expectations can help mitigate misunderstandings and build a more supportive relationship with management.

WORKING THROUGH IT

Now that we've identified the various sources of conflict, let's explore some strategies and approaches you can start using now to resolve these challenges when they arise:

- **Ground Rules:** Establishing ground rules for discussions is crucial. Ensure that respect is maintained at all times. Personal attacks should never be tolerated, no matter how heated the situation becomes. Additionally, confidentiality must be maintained. Discussions should remain private, and gossiping about conflicts at the water cooler will only exacerbate the situation.

- **Managing Emotions:** As a leader, you set the emotional tone. Stay calm and avoid becoming overly emotionally invested in the discussion. Encourage your team to practice emotional awareness, recognizing and understanding their own emotions. Foster an environment of active listening, focusing on solutions rather than dwelling on problems.

- **Open Communication:** Facilitate open communication by bringing everyone involved to the table. Even if parties can't immediately agree, creating a safe space for them to express their perspectives, concerns, and emotions can often lead to a resolution. Open dialogue can help uncover underlying issues that need addressing.

- **Validation:** Validating someone's feelings can be the gateway into a resolution. Acknowledge that someone is frustrated, angry, or hurt. This recognition can move the conversation in a positive direction and demonstrate that you respect their emotions and viewpoint.

- **Clear Expectations:** Ensure that everyone understands their roles, responsibilities, and expectations. Misunderstandings about job duties, goals, or performance evaluation criteria can often lead to conflict. Clear communication about these areas is essential for preventing misunderstandings and setting a foundation for cooperation.

- **Focus on Interests:** Encourage team members to focus on their underlying interests rather than sticking rigidly to their positions. Guide the conversation to explore potential solutions that address the interests of all parties involved. This approach can help find common ground and facilitate a more collaborative resolution process.

There may come a time when a conflict escalates beyond your direct control or intensifies to the point where it crosses personal or professional boundaries. When this happens, it's crucial to know when to escalate the issue. Consider involving higher management, HR, or mediation services as appropriate. Any conflict that involves harassment, discrimination, or any form of misconduct must be addressed immediately through the appropriate channels within your organization. I strongly encourage you to document all incidents meticulously and follow your organization's policies and procedures for handling such situations. Knowing when to involve other groups not only protects your team but also upholds the integrity and safety of your work environment.

PREVENTING FUTURE CONFLICT

To help prevent future conflict, it's essential to reflect on the lessons learned from past disputes. To start, you can ask questions such as, "What did we learn from this experience?" These challenging situations provide opportunities to clarify roles, establish or reinforce clear communication channels, and set the tone for continuous improvement.

Encourage feedback from your staff to understand their perspectives. Consider organizing workshops or training sessions focused on conflict management, negotiation techniques, and strategies like active listening and empathy.

These sessions can equip your team with the skills needed to handle conflicts constructively and maintain a positive work environment.

By implementing these strategies, you can cultivate a work culture that not only addresses conflicts effectively but also leverages them as opportunities for growth and improvement.

HEALTHY CONFLICT

In some situations, conflict can be healthy and even beneficial. As discussed in the previous chapter, strategies for cultivating a healthy workplace culture can help prevent and resolve conflict when it arises. Healthy disagreements, such as differing opinions on project approaches or revisiting longstanding practices, can foster increased productivity and overall job satisfaction. Embracing healthy conflict often acts as a catalyst for breaking out of cultural or organizational norms.

Employees who are satisfied with their office culture tend to demonstrate greater willingness to take risks, voice their opinions, and challenge the status quo. As a leader, you can nurture this environment by establishing a culture of safety, built on values like transparency, humility, and vulnerability. Here are some ways you can help establish and maintain a culture that promotes healthy conflict:

- **Set the tone:** Create an environment where team members feel secure in sharing their thoughts and challenging ideas without fear of reprisal. Encouraging open dialogue and healthy disagreements can lead to more innovative solutions, prevent groupthink, and enhance decision-making through critical thinking and collaborative problem-solving.

- **Lead by example:** Demonstrate transparency, humility, and vulnerability in your leadership. Share your own mistakes and lessons learned, show openness to feedback, and encourage others to do the same.

- **Foster a growth mindset:** Encourage your team to view conflicts as opportunities for learning and growth. A growth mindset promotes personal and professional development, encouraging individuals to see challenges as avenues for improvement and innovation.

CAN'T AVOID IT, BUT CAN GET THROUGH IT

Despite having the best hiring practices and building the healthiest possible workplace culture, conflict will inevitably arise. As a leader, it's important to accept this reality as a natural part of any workplace environment. By understanding the sources and recognizing early signs of conflict, you can proactively address challenges before they escalate. Following the guidelines outlined in this chapter equips you to navigate these complexities effectively.

Additionally, you are now prepared not only to manage current conflicts but also to prevent future ones. By viewing conflict as a potential catalyst for growth and improvement, you can foster a workplace environment that embraces healthy disagreements and promotes continuous learning and innovation.

Key Takeaways:

- **Inevitability of conflict:** Recognize that conflict is an inevitable aspect of any workplace, and being prepared is essential for effective leadership.

- **Sources and signs:** Understanding the common sources and early signs of conflict can enable you to proactively intervene before issues escalate.

- **Resolution strategies:** Employ strategies such as establishing ground rules, managing emotions, fostering open communication, and setting clear expectations to resolve conflicts effectively.

- **Know when to escalate:** If a conflict crosses personal or professional boundaries, it's critical that you escalate through proper leadership and HR channels, documenting everything along the way and following your organization's policies and procedures.

- **Preventative Measures:** Capture lessons learned to prevent future conflicts and consider team workshops and training to reinforce effective practices.

- **Embracing Healthy Conflict:** Recognize that not all conflicts are inherently bad; healthy disagreements can stimulate innovation and enhance job satisfaction, contributing to a dynamic and resilient organizational culture.

PART IV: PROCESS

In any I.T. department, we've learned that the **people** are crucial, but it's the **processes** that ensure everything runs smoothly and efficiently. This final part of the book shifts our focus to refining the processes that drive your team's success.

To remain competitive and innovative, it's essential to challenge the status quo and continuously seek improvements. Efficient processes help in maximizing productivity, reducing waste, and ensuring that your team can focus on what truly matters. Whether it's through better project management, optimizing workflows, or implementing new methodologies, refining your processes will lead to significant improvements in performance and outcomes.

By honing your process management skills, you'll not only streamline operations but also create a more agile and resilient organization.

Chapter 9:
The Dreaded Phrase

In previous chapters, I've shared various stories from my experience as an I.T. professional, highlighting key lessons that can be applied to your leadership journey. But of course, I myself am not immune to mistakes. Let me share a story where my lack of critical thinking resulted in a lot of wasted time:

Early in my career, I was assigned to install software updates and patches for my company's workstations. The procedure to complete the updates was established by my predecessor, who directly trained me before moving into a new role. The process was somewhat tedious, as it required manually installing updates on each individual computer. I went along with the procedure as written because that's the way I was taught.

Several months into my new role, I was still the manual patching guy – going around to each computer, installing the various updates one-by-one, occasionally wrestling with nagging feelings of being overwhelmed. Sometimes a patch would hang on a machine, and I'd be left waiting for it to finish. Other times I'd have a hard time working around the user's schedule to be able to get on the computer and run updates.

Then one day, I was introduced to *Jared*, a new colleague on our team. Jared was taking on the newly created role of Solutions Architect, where he would help drive our business goals into technical solutions. In other words, Jarrod would be our bridge between I.T. and operations. During an introductory meeting where I shared my duties, he (politely) questioned why I was manually installing these updates one at a time.

"Have you ever tried any automated patch deployment tools?" he asked.

To be fair, I had heard of them before, and had even seen them in action in a different organization. But who was this guy to tell me how to do my job, and in his first week no less?

"Well, yeah," I stammered defensively, looking down at my shoes before continuing. "But *Bob (my predecessor)* taught me to do it that way. He created the process… and I guess I've just been following that process."

Before I could stop it, the dreaded phrase slipped out of my mouth: "It's how we've always done it."

Jared smiled and nodded his head. We continued with the introductory pleasantries, and he went off to meet the rest of the team. Later that week, I called him up and asked him what software he's used in the past for automated patching, and he suggested a few solutions. While I was initially resistant to the change, and even a little defensive that the new guy called me out, we agreed to look into the solution. Jared was able to allocate some time to help implement the solution, and we ultimately rolled it out.

As expected, the automated patch deployment tool not only simplified the process of updating our workstations but also helped me to be more accurate and reliable – identifying machines that I missed or that weren't updated automatically. What had originally taken me days to accomplish could now be completed in just a few hours, with less effort to boot. The time saved freed me to focus on other areas that needed attention.

Looking back, I am reminded of two things – first, how great it is to have someone like Jared who can challenge conventional methods and come up with new, creative solutions. Second, how important it is to have a culture where the ability to challenge the established norms is welcomed and encouraged. By being open to new ideas and being willing to adapt, we were able to save significant time and money, opening up opportunities for new projects and tasks that were otherwise set aside for some unknown future date.

MOVERS AND SHAKERS

Looking back, I see that my experience is not a unique one. There have been countless times I've heard from staff – both I.T. and non-I.T. – the phrase "that's how we've always done it." This sentence is the perfect example of an underlying challenge within organizations, where deeply entrenched routines and practices can hinder growth, progress, and innovation. However, being able to challenge the status quo can often be the key to massive success.

In 2007, Steve Jobs announced the Apple iPhone, a device we all know revolutionized the smartphone industry. The iPhone featured a multitouch interface, which was in contrast to the physical keyboard and stylus-based interfaces. Many people doubted its potential success, with several famous writers and leaders questioning the shift to a touchscreen:

- David Platt, computer scientist and writer, wrote in his now-infamous article "Apple iPhone Debut to Flop, Product to Crash in Flames" how the design was "fundamentally flawed." He questioned the ability to have multiple functions in "one box," doubting the ability for a user to listen to music while surfing the web.

- Steven Levy, Senior Editor at Newsweek, expressed skepticism of the iPhone being able to get people to stop using their BlackBerrys and Treos (Palm device).

- Michael Kanellos, Senior Editor at CNET, questioned the usability of a touchscreen, saying it was no substitute for a keyboard when it comes to "serious e-mail or text messaging."

- Ed Colligan, CEO of Palm, was very dismissive of the iPhone as a threat to the smartphone market, sharing how he didn't think it would "be so easy for everybody," that "it's a tough space" (to be fair, as CEO of a competing company, he definitely had a vested interest in casting doubts over the iPhone).

Of course, as we all know, they were all wrong. According to Pew Research (2023), over 90% of US adults have a smartphone, and over 60% of them are iPhone users. While Android smartphones are more used worldwide, nearly all smartphones followed Apple's design of a sleek, rounded device, and of course – they all have a touchscreen now. Our smartphone-driven world would look vastly different had Apple opted to adhere to the status quo and retain physical keyboards or styluses in their device design. The shift to touchscreen technology revolutionized not only the way we interact with our mobile devices but also paved the way for innovations in mobile technology, app development, and user experience. By embracing innovation and challenging the norms of the time, Apple presented a transformational shift in the smartphone industry that continues to shape our digital landscape today.

Many organizations are still stuck in their old ways – following practices and procedures that were created 5, 10, or even 20 years ago. Despite the passing of time, the emergence of new technologies and solutions, and new perspectives entering the workforce, some still cling to their methods established long ago. The reluctance, or inability, to adapt and evolve with time will hinder growth, stifle innovation, and ultimately leave your organization behind your competitors. In today's rapidly evolving landscape, companies are eagerly looking to adopt anything they can to gain a competitive edge. If you're not using a tool or service to streamline your operations, rest assured, your competitor will.

The inability to let go of old ways and the phrase "that's how we've always done it" is a **process** problem. By not stepping out of the box, you are crippling your ability to properly leverage technology to make your life easier. Some real-world examples of this process I've encountered include:

- The use of manual paper to complete regular tasks, rather than using automated electronic forms and documents to streamline these processes;
- Manual I.T. involvement in rudimentary areas (such as setting up Zoom meetings or maintaining mailing lists);
- Reliance on outdated software or systems that lack modern functionality;
- Inefficient communication practices (such as email or in-person communications instead of more efficient team collaboration tools); and
- My favorite: sending emails back and forth as attachments, having the recipient edit, and then sending back to you (often repeating several times), resulting in several copies of the same file, rather than

using cloud-based collaborative tools like Microsoft SharePoint and OneDrive.

As I.T. professionals, it's our job to empower our customers (end users) to do their jobs as efficiently as possible. However, I've found over the years that I.T. staff can often be the source of resistance to change. Perhaps they fear change in general, as they're comfortable with the status quo and are hesitant to step out of their comfort zone. Maybe they are resistant to new technologies because they are unfamiliar with them. Or maybe they just aren't aware of the new technology because they're not putting themselves into positions to learn about them. Regardless of the reason, I've found that the resistance to change typically stems from three areas – **organizational culture**, **leadership dynamics**, and **employee mindset**. In the rest of this chapter, we'll examine each of these three areas and discuss how to break them down.

ORGANIZATIONAL CULTURE

Resistance to change often stems from deeply entrenched practices that have existed within an organization for years, or even decades. The comfort of familiarity can become a crutch of complacency. Longstanding employees who have been in their roles or departments for several years or even decades may cling to these practices that they either inherited or created themselves. New employees, meanwhile, are indoctrinated into existing practices and hesitate to suggest new ideas or ways to do things because the culture of the organization discourages such actions, whether subtly or blatantly. As a result, the organization plods along, continuing with the same practices and procedures without considering change, leaving itself lagging behind more agile competitors.

However, as leaders, we have the power to shake things up within our organization, no matter the size of our department or the company itself. We can lead by example, championing change. No matter how small, we can plant the seeds of innovation and adaptability. To start, identify areas within your sphere of influence that can benefit from improvement or automation, then take intentional steps to implement those changes.

Achieving this requires an intentional, innovative mindset that embraces thinking outside the box. Begin by exploring opportunities to automate certain processes. Conduct a cost-benefit analysis that compares the cost of maintaining the status quo with the investment needed to partially or fully automate a process. Be sure to consider not only the financial savings but also the time employees save, which can then be redirected to other tasks.

LEADERSHIP DYNAMICS

In more traditional hierarchical or autocratic organizational structures, decision-making authority is concentrated at the top, limiting the flow of new or innovative ideas from lower levels. While this setup may offer efficiency and clear lines of authority, it can also stifle creativity and hinder adaptability. Some leaders, driven by fear, prioritize stability over innovation, being overly cautious of the potential pitfalls and risks associated with change. As a result, employees are discouraged from proposing new ideas or challenging established norms, leading to stagnation and missed opportunities for growth.

On the flip side, leaders who encourage participatory decision-making and embrace diverse perspectives can unlock the full potential of their teams. By establishing an environment where all voices are heard and valued, these leaders empower individuals to challenge the status quo and contribute their unique insights. The best leaders embrace diversity in thought and approach, cultivating a culture of innovation that fosters a sense of ownership and commitment among their team members. In these organizations, innovation becomes a group effort, setting a tone of continuous improvement.

EMPLOYEE MINDSET

Many leaders I've worked with have shown resistance to change for various reasons – many of which are valid. Some fear the unknown—they're unsure what the future holds with this change and how it will personally impact them. Others express skepticism, wondering whether the new software will actually save them time, or if it will just create more work by changing something they've done the same way for 10 years. Concerns about job security are also common, with fears that new technology might automate their roles out of existence (a valid concern in all sectors, not just I.T.). Finally, some staff simply believe that things are fine as they are and see no need to disrupt the status quo.

As leaders, we must take an empathetic approach to these concerns. Many of them are valid and should be considered, especially as part of your overall strategy for the organization (remember chapter 5 - Strategy). Failing to properly plan for how changes will impact all parties can cause the change to be a failure – even if, at its core, it's a good idea.

A friend of mine once worked on a team of technicians supporting a midsized organization with around 200 employees. One of his team members was primarily responsible for managing the approximately 225 VOIP desk phones spread across the two floors that the company occupied in a large building. His tasks included moving phone lines, updating extensions, and managing the central device that connected all the phone lines.

A few years back, the company announced plans to outsource these tasks to a third-party provider as a cost-saving measure. Unfortunately, the I.T. Director failed to work with this employee during the transition or identify new responsibilities for him to take on. As a result, the technician found himself with a lot of free time on his hands.

A few months later, the I.T. Director left and was replaced by an outside hire. The new leader met with the staff to understand their roles, and it quickly became apparent that the technician assigned to manage the now-outsourced desk phones had little left to do. Within a month, he was let go due to a lack of responsibilities.

The importance of having a mindset that embraces change begins with us as leaders. Failure to do so will negatively impact both your department's effectiveness as well as your staff themselves.

One final note: if you have a staff member who is unable, or unwilling, to consider new ways of doing things, and despite your best efforts at validating their concerns and demonstrating the benefits of the change, they refuse to budge – then that person is probably not a good fit for your team. It's important to recognize that resistance to change can be a significant barrier to progress and innovation within your organization. As a leader, you must make difficult decisions to ensure your team remains agile and forward-thinking. While it's crucial to address concerns and provide support during transitions, there comes a point where persistent resistance can become detrimental. A staff member who is consistently unwilling to adapt can hinder the entire team's productivity and morale, creating a culture of stagnation and negativity. In such cases, it may be necessary to have candid conversations about their future with the organization, exploring whether they can find a role that better aligns with their comfort zone or if it might be best for them to seek opportunities elsewhere. Ensuring your team is composed of individuals who are open to growth and change is essential for fostering a dynamic and successful work environment.

EMBRACING CHANGE

As leaders, especially in the I.T. field, it's imperative that we not only embrace change but also champion it. In today's rapidly evolving technological landscape, remaining stagnant in traditional practices is simply not an option. Instead, we must cultivate a culture that values innovation, adaptability, and continuous learning. By encouraging a mindset that welcomes new ideas and challenges the status quo, we empower our teams to stay ahead of the curve, leveraging emerging technologies and strategies to better serve our organizations. This proactive approach drives real progress, enhances your team's efficiency, and helps maintain a competitive edge. Let's lead by example, inspire creative thinking, and cultivate an environment where change is embraced as an opportunity for growth and improvement.

Key Takeaways:

- **Challenge the Status Quo:** Questioning and challenging established routines and practices can lead to significant growth and innovation within your organization.
- **Embrace Change:** Being open to new ideas and willing to adapt is essential for saving time, money, and unlocking opportunities for new projects and tasks.
- **Organizational Culture:** Resistance to change often stems from deeply entrenched practices. Leaders must foster a culture that encourages innovation and adaptability.
- **Leadership dynamics:** Create an environment that encourages participatory decision-making and diverse perspectives to unlock your team's full potential.
- **Employee mindset:** Empathetically address employees' concerns about change, validating their fears and demonstrating the benefits of new approaches.

- **Not for everyone:** Leaders must be able to recognize staff members that are unable, or unwilling, to embrace change, and deal with them accordingly.

Chapter 10:
Empowering End Users

My friend (*Anthony*) once shared a story about his time as the I.T. manager for a medium-sized organization that managed several hotels and resorts. His primary responsibilities included overseeing projects and initiatives, supported by two additional staff members – one providing helpdesk and inventory support, and the other managing servers and the network environment.

Anthony recalled attending a leadership meeting with his fellow managers. During the meeting, one manager shared her computer screen on the conference room television to discuss an upcoming conference. Anthony noticed a folder on her desktop labeled "Conference Agenda," which contained numerous files named "v1," "v2," and so on. As she opened what she believed to be the latest version, another manager quickly pointed out that it wasn't the most recent one. They ended up spending several minutes searching for the correct version.

Later that day, Anthony approached the conference manager, (let's call him Brian), to discuss how he managed his agendas. Brian explained his process:

- He would start drafting the agenda, labeling it as "v1."

- He would send this draft to other conference planners for input, who would then return it with edits labeled as "v2," "v2-1," "v2-2," and so forth, depending on the number of revisions and contributors.

- This cycle would continue for several weeks or months, with each iteration creating a new version of the file.

Anthony immediately recognized the inefficiency of this process. The method led to confusion over which version was the latest, increased the risk of overwriting important updates, and resulted in significant time wasted tracking down the most recent file.

Anthony asked Brian if he was familiar with online collaborative tools that would allow multiple users to access and edit the same document simultaneously, eliminating the need for multiple versions. Brian admitted he wasn't aware of such tools. Anthony then inquired whether his predecessor had ever offered any advice or solutions for these kinds of issues.

"No, not really," Brian replied. "We just called him when something broke. We never really saw him, and he didn't contribute much during our leadership meetings, aside from updating us on the latest outage or technical issue."

THE OLD

Anthony's story is neither unique or new, and you've probably encountered a similar situation. The I.T. field has long struggled with effectively supporting users beyond merely fixing broken computers (and sometimes, even that's a challenge!). Many I.T. professionals follow a simple break-fix formula, where they emerge from their offices or cubicles to fix a malfunction, and then disappear back into their domain. This approach often means they are not involved in, or even familiar with, the daily operations of the organizations they support, leading to a lack of understanding about the impact of system failures or outages.

When giving presentations on this topic, I often reference the now infamous nerd character from the animated television series "South Park." In one episode, the characters play the video game World of Warcraft and face off against a godlike character who constantly defeats them. This character is portrayed as a middle-aged, balding man in a tiny apartment littered with pizza boxes and soda cans. His high-end computer is clean, but the rest of his desk is covered with crumbs and random CDs. The background is filled with loose clothes, piles of comic books, and nerdy statues. His unshaven, pimply face, adorned with crooked glasses, is a stark contrast to his fast mouse movements supported by a wrist brace.

Many people view I.T. professionals this way—as enigmatic characters, socially awkward, often perceived as the "guy in his mom's basement." Not particularly interested in building relationships with colleagues, they are often seen as weird and off-putting. They just make the magic happen, fixing computers, printers, or phones, and rarely appear otherwise.

This stereotype exists for a few reasons. First, it's deserved to some extent. As mentioned in an earlier chapter, stereotypes often contain a kernel of truth. Second, there has historically been a degree of segregation between I.T. and operations, largely due to the lack of technical understanding among non-I.T. staff. However, as a younger, more tech-savvy generation enters the workforce, this trend is changing. I often share a Venn diagram to illustrate the increasing overlap between I.T. and operations, showing how this intersection continues to grow over time.

THE NEW – AND THE WHY

As technology leaders, it's crucial to recognize the ongoing shift in our digital world. Where I.T. support once served primarily as technical first responders – patching and fixing issues – it is now evolving into a role of strategic partners who empower organizations to achieve their goals. Several factors contribute to this change, with one significant catalyst being the COVID-19 pandemic, which forced countless staff to work remotely. I.T. departments worldwide were called into action to help their users remain productive through those challenging years.

Conducting a survey on customer service revealed that post-COVID, consumers expect faster and better access to support. Whether it's ordering food, filing a claim on car insurance, or returning an item, customers now seek more ways to reach support—via email, live chat, phone, or text messages. Preferences varied among age groups, but the overall expectation for responsive and empathetic customer service was clear.

A few key statistics to consider:

- According to Statista, 67.1 percent of the world are internet users, up from 51.7 percent in June 2017 (Statista, 2024).

- According to a recent Pew Research Center survey, nearly 100% of Millennials in the United States use the internet, and 19% of them are smartphone-only internet users, meaning they rely solely on their smartphones for internet access and do not have broadband service at home (Pew Research Center, 2024).

- According to a Coresight Research survey, 54.3% of U.S. adults purchased groceries online in the past 12 months (Coresight Research, 2024).

One example of falling behind is the U.S. government. Despite citizens' expectations for more modern solutions, the federal government lags horrendously in software offerings. In 2019, the Government Accountability Office (GAO) reported on the use of legacy software systems, identifying ten department systems ranging from 8 years old to a surprising 51 years old. These outdated solutions cost a combined $337 million annually to operate and maintain. A follow-up report in 2023 revealed that eight of the ten departments had failed to adequately plan for their replacement. Some systems were no longer supported by the vendor, used outdated programming languages, or operated with known security vulnerabilities. Simply put, public sector leaders are failing to leverage technology effectively to serve their constituents, resulting in wasted tax dollars.

In Chapter 3, we discussed the importance of communicating at the right level. We know the next generation of staff entering the workforce will be more tech-savvy than ever, seeking new ways to work more efficiently and effectively. Supporting their evolving needs and communicating at their level of understanding are essential to meeting their requirements.

So why does this matter? Because as I.T. professionals, *we are in the customer service business*. Our staff and end users are our customers, and it's our job to empower them with the right technology to support their needs. Rather than simply handing over a laptop and a cell phone and telling them how to contact you for help, we should be looking for ways to empower them to be effective.

What does it mean to empower end users in the context of I.T.? Empowering end users means equipping them with the tools, knowledge, and resources they need to effectively use technology to perform their jobs. Let's take a deeper look into this concept.

WHAT IT IS (AND ISN'T)

So, what exactly is an empowered user, and how can you tell if you have them or not? Empowered users efficiently leverage technology to perform their duties. Adaptive by nature, they recognize that change is constant and are willing to embrace it. They can collaborate with I.T. staff, working as stakeholders or subject matter experts (SMEs) to create requirements (both functional and technical) and map these requirements into a solution. Finally, they understand that adopting new technology to meet their own needs, as well as the needs of the customers they serve, is no longer an option but a necessity. Most importantly, an empowered user can grasp and understand the relationship between I.T. and operations.

Let's touch briefly on what an empowered user is not. They are not the ultimate decider in technology strategy. It's important that both you in I.T. and the end users you serve work together as partners. Collaboration is much more effective than allowing one non-technical user to decide what software program you will use (and ultimately have to support!). Additionally, an empowered user does not have full administrative access to their computer. Giving free reign to their workstation is almost certainly against your policies (and if not, update your policies).

One way to look at empowering your end users is to consider how you can stop handholding them. Providing excellent service to your customers means helping them with their issues and taking the time to teach them what you did so they can be equipped to solve the issue themselves.

I briefly worked with a team of I.T. professionals who struggled with outdated practices. For instance, they managed numerous mailing lists manually. Instead of empowering staff to update these lists themselves, employees had to contact the I.T. helpdesk to make any changes. Additionally, this office frequently used Zoom for meetings, but the I.T. staff insisted on "managing" the licenses. By managing, I mean they kept control of the accounts and passwords, requiring end users to contact them to set up meetings. This process caused unnecessary delays, as employees had to submit tickets to I.T. just to schedule a meeting, rather than having their own accounts to create and host meetings directly.

For some meetings, the I.T. staff insisted on joining to "monitor" for unauthorized access and manage any slides that needed to be presented, creating an unnecessary layer of control. Unsurprisingly, this changed quickly when the new I.T. manager joined the team. There were a few bumps in the transition, as some less tech-savvy users felt I.T. support was necessary because they didn't know how to set up and manage their own virtual meetings. To address this, the new manager hosted a simple training session for anyone interested in learning how to run Zoom meetings. The session was recorded, and written user guides were provided to staff.

Empowering your users includes several key aspects:

- **Training and Education**: Provide regular sessions to ensure your users are proficient with the software and hardware they need to use. Offer resources like tutorials, online webinars, and user manuals that can help users troubleshoot common issues and even learn new functionalities on their own.

- **User-Friendly Options**: Leverage modern, intuitive, and user-friendly software solutions that minimize the learning curve and reduce reliance on technical support. Offer tools that allow your users to customize their work environments, such as email settings or application preferences.

- **Collaboration Tools**: Implement and support new tools that enable users to communicate and work more effectively, regardless of their location. Offer training on how to best use these tools to maximize their benefits.

- **Responsive Support**: Make sure your technical support is easily accessible and responds to their needs. Offer multiple channels for support, such as chat, phone, online portals, or email.

- **Autonomy and Independence**: Provide your users with a degree of autonomy to make decisions about the tools and technologies they use (within certain guidelines). Encourage innovation by supporting users who want to experiment with new technologies or solutions that could benefit their work.

By building an I.T. culture that empowers your end users, you will provide them with the knowledge, tools, and support they need to work effectively and independently.

This strategy will lead to a more efficient, innovative, and satisfied workforce, ultimately contributing to the success of your organization.

Key Takeaways:

- **Deserved Reputation:** Many I.T. staff have an often well-deserved negative reputation within their organizations.
- **Shifting Tide:** The new age of I.T. staff are strategic partners, empowering the staff they support with the best technology solutions and responsive support.
- **What It's Not:** Empowered users are not the sole decision-makers, do not have administrative access, and do not require constant handholding.
- **What It Is:** Empowering users involves providing comprehensive training and education, offering user-friendly options, utilizing the best collaborative tools, being responsive in support, and encouraging experimentation and innovation.

Chapter 11:
Let's Talk Projects

My friend (*Alice*) worked as the head of sales for a medium-sized software development company. Last year, their leaders decided to implement a new Customer Relationship Management (CRM) system to help streamline both their sales and customer service processes. Their initial goal was to increase sales efficiency, including upselling additional products or services, and to enhance customer satisfaction.

The project was spearheaded by Alice, who, working closely with her colleagues in sales, quickly found a vendor based on Google searches and recommendations from others in her field. Eager to move forward, Alice signed the contract with the CRM provider, and the project kicked off.

Excited to get started, Alice scheduled a kickoff meeting, inviting key members from her team who would help implement the solution. She prepared slides showcasing the features and benefits of the new system, along with a high-level overview of the steps required for implementation.

Alice also outlined the process changes necessary for the applicable staff and put together a timeline highlighting major milestones.

Feeling confident and energetic, Alice entered the kickoff meeting and began presenting her slides. She started by sharing their broad goals – "improve sales and customer management" – but failed to articulate clear objectives or metrics to measure the success of these goals. As she moved through her presentation, she revealed a simplified timeline with just five basic steps: procure the software, configure it on their servers, train users, update the website, and launch the solution. Finally, she concluded by listing the project team, which consisted solely of her team members, excluding staff from customer relations, accounting, or I.T.

Unfortunately, she immediately ran into problems. The first issue was related to procurement – when accounting saw the agreement drafted by the CRM company, they immediately rejected it due to several terms that were incompatible with their policies. This resulted in a lengthy contract negotiation phase that delayed the project by nearly six weeks. Finally, the contract was agreed upon and signed, and she could move forward.

Next, she went to the I.T. department, putting in a ticket to ask for their help in reviewing the options for installation (either on-site on their own servers, or using the CRM company's cloud-hosting service). She immediately received a call from an angry I.T. manager. He advised her that they were in the middle of their I.T. security audit, which had been scheduled over a year in advance, and would be unable to assist her until it was complete. Additionally, the manager expressed frustration about not being involved in the planning of this new deployment, as they could have advised on critical factors such as data migration, solution security, and ongoing support and maintenance costs.

It only got worse from there. Alice assumed her team could handle the transition to the new CRM solution without much issue. With this assumption, she simply sent them a PDF instruction manual on how to use the software, opting not to hold any training or Q&A sessions. Some staff ignored the document altogether, while others inundated Alice with phone calls, emails, chat messages, and office visits—asking countless questions about various features and functionalities.

Still, Alice pushed on. Her next headache came in the form of data migration, where a large amount of customer data was lost or corrupted. As a result, they had to go back to the CRM company for additional services, causing a run-up in costs. Determined, she opted to shift into a phased migration, launching the system with staff whose customer data was migrated without issue.

A few weeks into the soft launch, Alice checked in with the three sales staff assigned to use the new system. To her surprise, two of the three had abandoned it altogether and reverted to their old methods. The team felt unsupported and frustrated with the system, and in their words, the lack of training made it harder for them to do their work. They were wasting time navigating the confusing CRM menus. "It was faster to do it the old way," they shrugged, before turning back to their workstations.

Turning to the third staff member who was still using it, she asked how it was going. "Fine, I guess," came the hesitant reply. Alice tried to determine whether the new solution was effective, but without any established metrics for success, it was impossible to gauge if the CRM system was actually an improvement over their old practices.

Ultimately, after several months of trying to salvage the project, Alice's company decided to scrap it altogether. They incurred significant financial losses and wasted valuable time that could have been spent on more productive initiatives. Additionally, the project's failure brought with it a sense of skepticism towards new technology investments – no one wanted anything to do with them if they were going to be like this one!

THE PROBLEMS ARE LIMITLESS

I can't say I blame the employees for being frustrated in this situation. Even with our intention to break the mantra of "that's how we've always done it" that we went over in chapter 9, this project was doomed from the start. By failing to follow effective project management processes, Alice set herself – and her company – up for failure. This example is one of many I have seen, and perhaps you have witnessed similar situations over the years. Projects that don't leverage established processes often fail for a variety of reasons, including:

- **Lack of clear objectives**: In our story, Alice simply set a high-level, ambiguous goal to have "improved sales and customer management." This goal lacked any meaningful way to measure success. For example, what does "improved sales" mean? Is there a certain percentage increase they expect to see as a result of deploying the CRM system? What about "customer management"? How will they gauge their customers' satisfaction related to this new system? A lack of clear objectives can also lead to misaligned efforts, with team members working toward different, often conflicting, goals.

- **Poor planning**: Without a solid, vetted project plan, Alice's project faced resource shortages, massive delays, and budget overruns. By not accounting for all necessary resources (both human and financial), as well as not anticipating some obstacles, projects can become bogged down or fail completely due to unexpected challenges.

- **Ineffective communication**: Despite her intentions, Alice didn't effectively communicate her project's goals, timelines, and needs to the right people. This led to delays, increased costs, and ultimately the failure of the project altogether. By not keeping team members and stakeholders informed about key decisions, changes, or updates, confusion will run rampant. Additionally, some may end up feeling disconnected or ignored, lowering their engagement with the project. Overall, poor communication can severely undermine project coordination and cohesion, making it difficult or impossible to achieve the stated goals.

- **Resistance to change**: We had a whole chapter on this (chapter 9), but it's important to reiterate how this resistance can negatively affect a project's success. Some hesitation may be valid – due to the three main variables we discussed (organizational culture, leadership dynamics, or employee mindset). It doesn't help if your company has a track record of failure with projects. Staff had every right to resist changes when they were left unsupported in the training process, communication was minimal, and they lacked any valid reason to use the new system in the first place.

- **Risk management**: By not accounting for risks, Alice was forced into reactive mode, constantly putting out fires instead of advancing the project. She encountered avoidable delays with accounting and I.T., and also faced technical issues during the migration of customer data. Failing to identify risks and plan for them leaves projects vulnerable to unexpected issues that can derail progress.

BEING INTENTIONAL

Effective project management is not just a requirement for I.T. departments – it's an essential practice for the health of any organization. In our story above, Alice's failure to launch the new CRM system had nothing to do with the technology itself. It stemmed from a failure in following a good project management **process**. There are many books, programs, guides, and certifications out there to help you become a great project manager, but it's important to understand *why* before learning *how*. Let's look at some benefits of good project management:

- **Achieving your goals and objectives**: This one is probably the most obvious. Good project management starts with setting clearly defined goals and objectives that are aligned with your organization's strategic vision or plan (remember chapter 5 - Strategi). By creating a detailed roadmap with measurable milestones and goals, the focus is more clear on the desired outcome. Having a structured approach in your planning and executing of the project, as well as monitoring progress and measuring success, you can drastically increase the likelihood of project success.

- **Effective resource management**: In this context, the term "resource" includes human, financial, and material resources. Planning and allocating resources effectively can ensure that team members aren't overburdened, will help to minimize project overruns, and ensure that you have what you need when you need it. Effective resource management will help your project be completed on time and within budget.

- **Improved communication**: This was also important enough to have an entire chapter dedicated to it (chapter 3). As leaders, promoting open and transparent communication with all parties involved in the project is essential for its success. By providing regular updates, clear reporting structures, and clearly defined communication channels, you can ensure that everyone stays informed about your project's progress, any issues that arise, or other essential information. This will also help build trust and relationships with your stakeholders and other staff in your organization, which will be helpful for future projects.

- **Managing risk**: This is an often overlooked step but can also be the most disastrous. Risk management includes identifying risks to your project's success (whether financial, schedule, communication, or technological), assessing the likelihood and impact of these risks occurring, and clearly outlining steps to mitigate the risks throughout the project.

- **Scope creep**: Scope creep occurs when a project's scope expands beyond what was originally intended. These changes can sometimes be beneficial – let's use an example: suppose you're deploying a new software solution, and halfway through, you realize that adding an unselected module would actually be beneficial. By expanding the scope to include this module, you could save significant time and money. However, scope creep can also derail a project by introducing too many new requirements, functions, solutions, or processes. To manage scope creep effectively, establish a documented and well-understood change management process where all proposed changes are carefully reviewed and either approved or denied

- **Increased "customer" satisfaction**: Remember, in the I.T. field, your customers are the employees, end users, and stakeholders within your organization. By delivering projects on time and within budget, you can improve your "customer" satisfaction.

- **Better productivity**: Healthy project management leads to increased productivity as projects will be completed on time and within budget. This increase in productivity will also allow teams to take on more projects, further contributing to the overall performance of your organization.

- **Better morale**: When everyone understands their roles and responsibilities, receives regular feedback, and feels valued for their contributions to the project, their morale will improve. As we discussed in chapter 7 (Building the Culture), this leads to increased motivation, engagement, and overall job satisfaction. These motivated team members are more likely to work effectively and contribute to project success.

- **Competitive advantage**: Finally, leveraging efficient project management processes enables you and your organization to respond quickly to market changes, bringing new and innovative products or services to your market faster.

GETTING STARTED

OK great, we've seen the pitfalls of poor project management, as well as the benefits of good project management. How do we get started?

First, we need to understand where we are currently. In other words, the first step in implementing effective project management is to conduct a thorough assessment of your current practices. This involves identifying the strengths and weaknesses of your existing processes, tools, and capabilities. You might realize that you have *zero* existing processes – that's fine, we all have to start somewhere. Understanding what is working well and what isn't working so well will allow you to prioritize areas for improvement. You can also ask your colleagues, leaders, or other team members for feedback. Finally, review past project performance to identify patterns of success or failure.

Next, begin to implement best practices for project management. Reflecting on Alice's story at the beginning of this chapter, we see some essentials: establishing detailed project plans, defining clear project scopes, setting goals and detailed measurements for success, creating stakeholder communication plans, managing risks, and monitoring progress.

If nobody on your team is familiar with these practices, look at taking courses in project management. Certifications like COMPTIA's Project+ or offerings from the Project Management Institute (PMI) are great options. These programs provide training on the essential topics discussed above – helping you successfully plan, execute, monitor, and close out projects. Most larger organizations employ full-time project managers who have the certifications and experience to manage their projects (which is a great career choice if you're interested!).

Setting the right goals for your project is key. Using the **SMART (Specific, Measurable, Achievable, Relevant, Time-bound)** framework is common in project management. Following this acronym, SMART goals can give you clear direction and criteria for success. **Specific** goals define exactly what needs to be done; **measurable** goals help you track progress and success; **achievable** ensures you're setting realistic goals and not biting off more than you can chew; **relevant** ensures you're aligned with the broader goals of your organization (refer back to chapter 5 on strategy); and **time-bound** helps you set deadlines for the project and specific milestones.

Finally, there is a wide range of project management software available that can significantly improve your ability to manage projects. These tools offer features such as communication, collaboration, and task tracking. Some popular solutions include Trello for visual task management, Microsoft Project for more detailed scheduling and resource management, and Jira for tracking issues and managing agile projects. However, the **process** is more important than the tool itself. These software products should serve as enhancements to your established project management processes, not dictate them. If you're considering a software product to help manage projects, look for specific features that align with your needs and existing processes. Ultimately, the effectiveness of any tool will depend on how well your team adopts and uses it.

FAILING FORWARD

So, you've established the best project management processes and are doing everything perfectly. You've got great goals with measurable metrics, a solid communication plan, completed a thorough risk assessment, and have done everything you can to ensure your project is a success.

Guess what? Some of them will still fail. Often external dependencies can be the cause. Unforeseen factors will creep in at one point or another. For instance, if you're relying on a third-party vendor for a deliverable and they suddenly go out of business, your project could be canceled or, at the very least, significantly delayed. Market conditions might shift, rendering your project no longer beneficial to your organization's customers. Your company's financial situation could change unexpectedly, leading to cuts in the funds previously allocated to your effort. Or – as we've seen more recently – a global pandemic might shut down the world for an extended period, bringing projects to a standstill.

Many of the factors listed above are uncontrollable – certainly that was the case with COVID – but even projects that fail due to reasons within your control are not a complete loss. These failures can serve as powerful lessons for growth and improvement. After the conclusion of a project that goes sideways, I recommend conducting a thorough review to identify what contributed to its failure. Gather input from all team members and stakeholders to gain an understanding of what happened. Document these lessons and use them to update your organization's project management practices, helping to prevent similar issues in the future.

Another "failure" in a project might occur when you're prototyping a new solution. You buy (or develop) a software product to improve your processes, only to find after testing that it's not really needed. Guess what? That's a win! You've achieved your goal. This 'failure' is actually a success because you now have a clearer understanding of what your organization truly needs.

Having an organizational culture that actually embraces failure as a positive activity can foster innovation and build resilience among staff (refer to chapter 7, Building the Culture). Embracing the potential of failure can empower your team members to take risks that could pay off massively. As leaders, you play a critical role by openly discussing failures (including your own), pointing out the lessons learned, and even acknowledging or rewarding attempts to innovate, even when they don't succeed. Having a culture of safety where team members feel secure in taking risks and aren't afraid of failure will help them feel supported and empowered. They are more likely to push boundaries, suggest ideas outside of your organization's cultural norms, and explore new ideas.

The concept of project management is not unique to the field of information technology. However, many nontechnical leaders or stakeholders are hesitant to get involved in a technical project, as they fear they might not understand all the details. But the **processes** for effective project management transcend all areas of business. By following proven project management **processes**, you'll be taking a massive leap forward towards success for yourself, your team, and the company as a whole!

Key Takeaways:

- **Fail to plan, plan to fail:** Not following effective project management **processes** will almost certainly result in project failure.

- **Multitude of reasons:** Poor planning, ineffective communication, resistance to change, and an inability to manage risks are just a few of the reasons why projects fail.

- **Intentionality:** Benefits of good project management include effective resource management, improved communication, controlled scope creep, increased customer satisfaction, better productivity, higher morale, and maintaining a competitive edge.

- **Effective communication:** For those new to project management, seek out courses or certifications, set S.M.A.R.T. goals, communicate regularly with stakeholders, and leverage project management software tools to ensure success.

- **Failure isn't always bad:** A failed project can be a valuable learning experience, capturing critical lessons and fostering growth for your organization.

Chapter 12:
The Journey Ahead

If you've made it this far in the book, thank you! It is my hope that these chapters and pages will serve you wherever you are in your career journey. By breaking down your technological challenges to the root **people** or **process** problems (or both), you'll be well-equipped to address them. Whether you're just starting out in the field of information technology, a new manager eager to lead your team successfully, an experienced director looking to enhance your leadership skills, or a non-technical senior leader hoping to better support your I.T. manager and their team, I hope the lessons in the previous chapters will be of great help.

Before we wrap things up, I have one last short story to tell – one a little more personal than the rest. While writing this book, a colleague I frequently worked with retired on short notice. This person was well known and well respected in our field. While everyone wished him well, the elephant in the room was who would fill the now-vacant position. It was well-paying for our industry and offered excellent benefits.

I was talking with one of my team members – who happens to be qualified for the job. I was curious if he'd be interested in applying for the role.

"Nah," came his casual reply. "I'm really happy working here, and I don't want to mess that up. I like my job – I enjoy what I'm doing, I feel supported, the work-life balance is good… I'm not going anywhere."

Wow.

Now, I know this sounds like a humble brag (and maybe it is, a little bit). But I can tell you that as a leader, there is no greater thing to hear from your staff. To hear from your team members that they are happy with their roles, that they feel respected, supported, and actually enjoy the work they are doing – this is the ultimate peak of leadership achievement. Not the sales goals, not the quarterly profit margin, not the completed projects.

As leaders, we should all strive for this. We should support, serve, and empower our staff to perform their jobs. Providing a healthy, supportive, fun, encouraging, and hard-working environment is key. Serving those around us offers a greater reward than any salary could ever provide.

And to be clear, he might change his mind and go for that job. He has every right to, and as a leader, if that's his personal career goal, then I will support and encourage him. Will it be hard to lose him, since he's a great asset? Absolutely. But it's more important that we support our staff in fulfilling their professional goals. The true measure of any leader isn't the rewards or accolades they receive, but the success and satisfaction of their team. When they are recognized, when they get promoted (not everyone will stay, and that's a good thing), when they are rewarded or acknowledged for their efforts – that's a win for you as well.

And that's why I wrote this book. As a leader, you can transform your organization – or, at the very least, your sphere of influence. Following the principles outlined in this book – to focus on **people** and **process** – will position you for success.

Take time to reflect on your career path so far, being brutally honest about your strengths, just as important, your weaknesses. If you're struggling with communication, write it down and commit to working on it. Maybe you're having issues with self-confidence and delegating tasks — note it and create a plan to improve. If you're a senior leader and recognize a lack of oversight in your technology department, acknowledge it. Often quoted around the new year, Pearson's Law states, "That which is measured improves. That which is measured and reported improves exponentially." Measuring where you currently are and comparing it to where you want to be is the first step.

Let's revisit what we've covered in this book. We began by examining the challenges organizations face with their I.T. departments. Some interesting, and maybe humorous, examples were shared that shine a light on the struggles many face. In chapter 2 we narrowed down the source of these challenges – namely, how these are related to **people** and **process** problems. By focusing on the areas of **people** and **process**, we can better lead our technical teams.

Next, we explored leadership essentials, starting with communication – an essential but often lacking skill among I.T. professionals – and outlined tangible strategies for improvement in this area. We then discussed delegation in chapter 4 – looking at why some managers hesitate to delegate, and practical steps to begin doing so. Finally, we covered strategic planning, emphasizing the importance of a proactive rather than reactive leadership approach.

In the next section, we dove into the **people** aspect of leadership. We provided a detailed roadmap for recruiting the best talent for your organization in chapter 6. However, hiring the right **people** is not enough. In the next chapter, we learned about the critical importance of building a healthy work culture. Finally, recognizing that interpersonal conflict is inevitable, chapter 8 addressed sources of conflict and specific strategies to navigate (not avoid) disagreements in the workplace.

In the final chapters, we turned our attention to leadership **processes**. We discussed how to challenge the status quo and tackle the infamous phrase "that's how we've always done it" in chapter 9. We then presented a perspective shift on I.T., highlighting how we can empower our end users to perform their duties without hindering them. Finally, in chapter 11, we provided a high-level, but important look into the critical need for effective project management.

The book is structured so that individual chapters in parts 2, 3, and 4 can be picked up and read independently. If you or someone you know is struggling with delegation, dive into chapter 4 for quick tips (or a refresher!). However, the most important takeaway that I hope you, the reader, have from this book is that we must shift our perspective when addressing technology problems. By focusing first on the **people** and **process** issues underlying the challenges you face, you'll be on the right track to lead and support the technology needs of your organization.

LOOKING FORWARD

These days, writing a book about technology can be a challenge. During the several months it took to complete these chapters, artificial intelligence (AI) has emerged as the next great advancement in the technology field, with tools like ChatGPT becoming as common as Google for many. In the world of I.T., adaptability is a necessity. New tools, methodologies, and challenges emerge daily, requiring I.T. professionals to be agile, flexible, and responsive. Being rigid – both in approach and method – can render you obsolete. Embracing new technologies and pivoting quickly due to emerging innovations or market changes will help you succeed in your career.

But at the end of the day, these new technologies are still just that – tools to help make our lives better (well, we hope). No amount of high-tech gadgets, gizmos, widgets, or software will replace the need for intentional, healthy, proactive leadership. By adopting a leadership approach that focuses on the **people** and **processes** in your organization, you'll be on the right track to success, regardless of the technology you use.

Leadership – especially in the I.T. field – can be a demanding but deeply rewarding journey. I challenge you to embrace these opportunities and step into your role with confidence! Set goals for yourself and your team. Encourage them to think big and aim high. Give them a sense of direction and purpose, maintaining a proactive approach rather than a reactive one. Make sure you never get too busy to be there to support your team members. Give them (and yourself) chances to learn – explore new opportunities, attend conferences, and grab coffee with a mentor (or become a mentor yourself and invite someone to coffee!).

Each day will bring new challenges, but also opportunities for growth. Stay on the path – don't be deterred by setbacks but look to them as learning experiences. Continue to build a great team and encourage them to adopt a similar approach. Be curious, foster open dialogue, be open to new ideas, and always be learning and improving. Set goals and take action to achieve them, encouraging those around you to do the same.

Your journey towards excellence is a lifelong commitment. Celebrate your wins but stay focused on the future. Be humble and open to feedback, always striving for excellence. The impact you can make as a leader extends far beyond your immediate work. Your success will inspire and uplift those around you, creating longstanding waves of change well beyond what you can see. Your efforts will not only enhance your own life but will also have a lasting impact on your team, your organization, and your community.

So, act now – commit to your journey of leadership excellence!

It's a new day.

For more insights, resources, and to continue the conversation, visit richard-blalock.com

Made in the USA
Las Vegas, NV
28 October 2024